GREAT BRITISH
PASSENGER SHIPS

GREAT BRITISH
PASSENGER SHIPS

WILLIAM MILLER

To Ian & Lauren Wright,
dearest friends, cherished shipmates & equal fans of bygone times

First published 2010

The History Press
The Mill, Brimscombe Port
Stroud, Gloucestershire, GL5 2QG
www.thehistorypress.co.uk

British Library Cataloguing in Publication Data.
A catalogue record for this book is available from the British Library.

ISBN 978 0 7524 5662 1

Typesetting and origination by The History Press
Printed in Great Britain
Manufacturing managed by Jellyfish Print Solutions Ltd

CONTENTS

FOREWORD

I was born in the maritime city of Liverpool, where I spent most of my early childhood, growing up to be fascinated by the shipping on the River Mersey. I soon learned to recognise the various funnel markings and house-flags of the port's shipping companies.

My mother's family had arrived by sea to Liverpool in a ship called the *Marietta* from their homeland in Montenegro, a tiny kingdom in the Balkans. Liverpool has for generations welcomed emigrants from many countries of the world. My family was fortunate to be well educated, speaking several languages including English and with funds to purchase a fine Georgian house in the city which overlooked a beautiful park. My maternal grandmother, Marie-Louise Myers, had Eleanor Rathbone, a suffragette, as a best friend. The Rathbone family were probably the most prominent dynasty in Liverpool, and the Rathbone Shipping Company imported grain and cotton from the United States. The company later became trading agents for the giant East India Company.

Liverpool's shipping companies had some of the best-known names of the nineteenth and twentieth centuries: names like Cunard, Canadian Pacific, White Star, Ellerman, Blue Funnel, Bibby and the Anchor Line – to name just a few associated with the port. I have vivid childhood memories of being taken down to the docks to see the British passenger liners at Prince's Landing Stage and of often being taken aboard to see those floating palaces of opulence. My grandfather told me of his brother who had sailed in the infamous *Lusitania* in May 1915, which was torpedoed and sunk off Kinsale in Ireland with a loss of 1,198 lives. The story sent shivers down my spine.

The Liverpool Docks were nearly eight miles in length – one of the biggest ports in the world. I well remember seeing the great Cunarders, ships such as the *Carinthia*, *Saxonia*, *Franconia* and *Sylvania*, which crossed the great Atlantic Ocean to Canada. I witnessed the final sailing of the *Britannic*, the last ship to be owned by the White Star Line, on a bitterly cold and gloomy 25 November 1960, as she sailed from Liverpool for New York. With her Red Ensign proudly fluttering in a strong crosswind, hundreds of people cheered her on from the quayside, saying a final farewell, with proud British hearts beating. It is an image that has remained with me all of my life.

My own connection with the sea began at the time of my birth and christening. I was fortunate to have a godfather who was to become the chairman of the largest British passenger line, the Peninsular & Oriental Steam Navigation Company, the iconic P&O.

My earliest memory of travelling by sea was in the 1950s when I accompanied my parents out to South Africa in ships of the Union-Castle Line. This continued well into the 1960s on a fairly regular basis and especially during the bleak British winters. Union-Castle ships left Southampton at four o'clock on a Thursday afternoon for the thirteen-day voyage via Las Palmas, southbound to Cape Town, where the majority of the passengers disembarked. We always remained on board for the onward passage via Port Elizabeth and East London to Durban, where we stayed at the famous Edward Hotel on Marine Parade. The sea voyage saw the same families travelling every year. We normally sailed southbound in the *Windsor Castle* where my parents dressed formally for dinner each evening, apart from sailing day and Sunday. Our return to Southampton, sailing on Tuesday from Durban and via Cape Town and Madeira, was usually in the *Pendennis Castle*.

In 1972 it was arranged for me, through my godfather, to travel as a Special Interest Lecturer on the *Arcadia* and, in the following year, on the *Orsova*. The *Orsova* was in fact on her final cruise before being taken out of service and going to the breakers. In 1974 I sailed in *Oriana* for a three-week voyage to the West Indies, returning to Southampton. On the outward voyage, the ship encountered Hurricane Fifi, one of the deadliest hurricanes ever recorded. There were damages throughout the ship and hundreds of passengers were confined to their cabins. It is only when you experience this kind of bad weather at sea that you are thankful for a well-built British ship and her highly trained officers and crew. Afterwards, I went seven times around the world in P&O ships. Four of these trips were aboard the iconic *Canberra*.

My dear friend Bill Miller and I first met, in fact, on the *Canberra* in October 1980. I was riveted by his lectures, especially when he spoke of the many ships I sailed on over the years. This book relives that great era of travel by sea in British passenger ships, when you could sail to the four corners of the world in a British ship, with a feeling of security and total permanence. You were travelling under the Red Ensign and when Britannia still ruled the waves. You will be captivated by ships now sadly gone into the mists of time and the very size of the British liner fleet. They really were the best of British and will, through this book, be forever remembered.

Howard Franklin
Shropshire
Spring 2010

ACKNOWLEDGEMENTS

I recall countless Atlantic crossings and leisurely cruises on which I met fellow passengers and loyal crew-members who sailed earlier on some of the ships mentioned in these pages. They had crossed the North Atlantic on the likes of the legendary *Queen Mary and Queen Elizabeth*, cruised on the *Andes*, sailed to Cape Town on the *Edinburgh Castle* and made the long journey out to Melbourne and Sydney in the *Iberia*. And, of course, there were the select few who sailed the more remote ships such as a Fyffes passenger-cargo ship to Jamaica, Blue Star to Rio and Buenos Aires, Blue Funnel out to Hong Kong and British India from Bombay to the Persian Gulf. They have all added to my personal fascination and understanding of the great British passenger fleet. Warmest thanks to each of them.

I am also especially grateful to The History Press for taking on this title and subsequent volumes in this series. I am most grateful to Howard Franklin for his evocative and reflective Foreword and to Robert Lloyd for the splendid colour covers, which in themselves remind us of the golden age of British ocean liners. And a great nod of thanks and respect to Don Stoltenberg, a wonderfully talented maritime artist, and himself a great keeper of ocean liner history and style.

Very special thanks to friends, enthusiasts and fellow collectors who shared insights, anecdotes and, mostly, prized photographs. Among the first-class 'crew' are the late Frank Braynard, Tom Cassidy, Richard Faber, the late John Gillespie, Michael Hadgis, Abe Michaelson and Albert Wilhelm

Other important loyal and devoted 'crew-members' include Ernest Arroyo, John Bolton, the late P.J. Branch, the late Douglass Campbell, Michael Cassar, Jim Clench, Anthony Cooke, Luis Miguel Correia, Charles Cotton, the late Frank Cronican, Des Cox, Tony Dent, Billie Ellis, John Ferguson, Richard Gibson, the late Betty Green, Charles Haas, Brian Hawley, Clifford Hocking, Pine Hodges, the late F. Leonard Jackson, Terry Johnson, Lindsay Johnstone, Dr David Kirkman, Des Kirkpatrick, Peter Knego, Anthony La Forgia, Robert Neal Marshall, Ove Neilsen, the late Victor Newman, Tony Ralph, Robert Pabst, the late Ron Peach, Selim San, the late Leslie Shaw, the late Willie Smith, the late G.D. Watt, Commodore Ronald Warwick, Steffen Weirauch and the late Len Wilton.

Companies and organisations deserving of acknowledgement include Canadian Pacific Steamships, the Carnival Corporation, Crystal Cruises, Cunard, Furness-Bermuda Line, Moran Towing & Transportation Co., the Ocean Liner Council at the South Street Seaport Museum P&O, the Port Authority of New York and New Jersey, Queen Mary Hotel, St Helena Shipping Co., Snowbow Productions, the Steamship Historical Society of America, the World Ocean & Cruise Liner Society and the World Ship Society.

Humble apologies to anyone that I have overlooked.

INTRODUCTION

On an overcast morning in September 2009, the mighty 1,132ft-long *Queen Mary 2*, inbound from New York, berthed at Southampton's newest cruise facility. The Cunard flagship docked bow-first and, among her nearly 2,600 passengers, I was one of the first off, being in the 'self-help' group so as to make an early train up to Shropshire. The reception, the baggage handling and even the taxi access could not have been more efficient. It was my first experience at the fourth terminal of the expanded cruise facilities at Southampton. Aptly, the new berth was named Ocean Terminal.

Officially opened just months before, in May, the $35 million terminal – created in a joint venture between the Port of Southampton and Carnival UK (who owns Cunard, among others) – is a response to Southampton's (and Britain's) booming passenger ship business. In 2008, the historic port handled 289 cruise calls, representing a processing of some 900,000 passengers. That figure represented a doubling of the amount of passengers from just four years earlier, and was expected to hit the million mark by 2010. Named the Ocean Terminal, it is a supplement to the three existing cruise facilities at the port: Berth 101, Berth 106 and the Queen Elizabeth II Terminal. The new facility is more accurately Berth 46 in the Ocean Dock.

Ocean Dock and Ocean Terminal are rather iconic names to the Port of Southampton. The previous Ocean Terminal was a rather grand, late Art Deco creation that, because of the Second World War, was actually not completed until 1950. Done in blonde, burl woods on the inside and painted white on the outside, it had sweeping waiting rooms, baggage areas, a flower shop, newspaper and magazine stand, spectator galleries and, most conveniently, a ground-level link to trains to and from London. Passengers could be at Waterloo station in less than two hours. Business boomed in the 1950s and '60s, for example, when legendary liners, such as the *Queen Mary* and *Queen Elizabeth*, the *Andes*, *Oriana* and *Canberra* called regularly. Passengers – including small armies of celebrities on the Atlantic crossings – then often travelled with trunks, servants, pets, even big American cars. Myself, I last recall using the Ocean Terminal when returning from a cruise in October 1980 on board *Canberra*.

Sadly, in 1983, that original Ocean Terminal fell victim to the wreckers' ball. It should have been saved and today would have been ideal for re-use by contemporary liners, including the likes of the mighty *Queen Mary 2*. After demolition, the idea was to rebuild the site as a cargo terminal, but that never came to pass and instead, of all things, it served for a time as a scrap-metal depot and mooring for laid-up out-of-work ships. Big oil tankers and boxy car carriers, sitting out slump phases in their respective trades, have often used that original Ocean Terminal berth.

And while Southampton reportedly had future expansion plans, the Ocean Terminal is a grand reminder, a link, to the golden age of British passenger shipping. This book is meant to be an aide-memoire, perhaps evocatively and reflectively, of the days when passengers travelled to Southampton to board the likes of Canadian Pacific to Quebec City, Royal Mail to Rio, Union-Castle to Cape Town and P&O to Sydney. The British passenger ship fleet of the twentieth century was like no other. This is one more great nod to a grand, but largely bygone, era.

Bill Miller
Secaucus, New Jersey
Spring 2010

one

EDWARDIAN TRIUMPHS & SPLENDOURS

In grand style, the Duchess of Roxburgh travelled to Newcastle on 26 September 1906. Newcastle was then one of the greatest shipbuilding centres in the world, a distinction then shared with the Clyde and with Belfast over in Northern Ireland. The British were the master shipbuilders as well as designers and marine engineers. Even the Germans, along with the Dutch, the Belgians and the distant Italians, were building ships, including passenger liners, in British shipyards. German shipyards would soon acquire great skills themselves, however, and offer fierce competition in a matter of years, in that murky twilight before the onset of the First World War. But on that early autumn day, the Duchess had come to the Swan, Hunter & Wigham Richardson shipyard to name the largest, fastest and, according to many, the most luxurious ocean liner yet created. Britain was at its zenith.

Along with her vast geographic empire, the British flag flew from more ships than any other. Just three years before, in 1903, there were 20,000 ships flying national colours – 10,000 still under sail and another 10,000 using steam. The British fleet totalled a staggering 10 million gross tons. By 1914, half of the entire world's merchant fleet was under the British flag.

Liverpool based, the great Cunard Line was to many the largest and most prestigious shipping firm anywhere. They owned and operated some of the greatest and grandest passenger liners on the very prestigious, but also very competitive, North Atlantic route to North America, especially to New York. Actually, Cunard had been facing furious competition from another British-flag but American-owned company, the White Star Line, as well as a quartet of very powerful German super-liners (the 14,300 grt *Kaiser Wilhelm der Grosse*, *Kronprinz Wilhelm*, *Kaiser Wilhelm II* and, finally, the 19,300 grt *Kronprinzessin Cecilie*), owned by the Bremen-headquartered North German Lloyd. Looking to the future, Cunard had to compete and retain its following of Atlantic passengers. Consequently, and prompted by large loans from London, Cunard decided to build the largest and fastest liners afloat, the *Lusitania* and *Mauretania*, both commissioned in 1907. They soon made headlines on both sides of the Atlantic.

Together with Cunard, and by the turn of the century, the White Star Line was considered something of a pinnacle, a grand benchmark in British ocean liner services. They were noted for their fine ships, reliable services and high standards of on board care and service. They were also keen competitors for national prestige and honour but mostly for a great share of the very lucrative transatlantic passenger trade.

White Star's *Oceanic*, completed in 1899, was then the largest liner afloat. She was 17,200 tons and ranked as the first liner to exceed 700ft in length. Seen as a marvel of British design, engineering and construction, she could carry up to 1,700 passengers, some of them in palatial, gilded, upper-deck luxury. But even larger ships were in White Star's future. There were the 21,000-ton sisters *Celtic* and *Cedric*, built in 1901–03, and then, larger still, two near sisters of the earlier pair, the 24,000-ton *Baltic* and *Adriatic*. This latter pair came into service in 1904.

The twin-screw, 19-knot *Oceanic* ranked also, in 1899, as the most expensive liner to date, costing a staggering $3½ million. She was also rated as the most popular liner on the very busy Liverpool–New York run. Her greatest profits came from her lower-deck steerage passengers, of course. The late Mary McGuire came to America through the infamous Ellis Island in 1910. She crossed from Queenstown in steerage on board the *Oceanic*. 'It was really very uncomfortable, down in those crowded quarters. Most of us had never even seen the ocean before and here we crossing the great and very wide, it seemed, Atlantic Ocean,' she recalled in an interview in the early 1970s. 'But we wanted to go to America, the New World, and have greater opportunity. The voyage on the *Oceanic* was, as I remember, worth it at any cost.'

Capped by two very tall funnels and carrying three tall masts, the *Oceanic* may have lost rank but remained in service until the dramatic summer of 1914. The First World War started in August and, along with many others, the liner was converted by the British Admiralty into an armed merchant cruiser. Her military days were short-lived, however. A month later, on 9 September 1914, she was wrecked up in the Shetland Islands. All but abandoned, she was later gradually scrapped, until the final remains were removed in 1924.

White Star directors, and therefore their designers, were not interested in high speed and so were indifferent to the prized Blue Riband. Instead, they emphasised comfort on the high seas and reliability, and even a sense of familiarity to travellers. The great success of the *Oceanic* led rather quickly to successively larger and more luxurious ships. This time for the exterior, however, the company designers opted for twin funnels and no less than four masts. The masts were to be reminders to the public of the great sailing ships of the bygone nineteenth century. Consequently, the ships also appeared conservative

End of her days: the *Celtic* aground at Queenstown in a photograph dating from December 1928. *(Richard Faber Collection)*

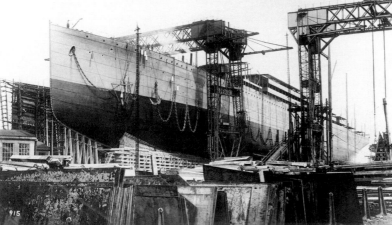

Above, from top
White Star Line's 17,200grt *Oceanic* was for a time, between 1899 and 1901, the largest liner afloat. She is seen berthed at Liverpool. *(Richard Faber Collection)*

The *Cedric* resting on the ways on 21 August 1902, prior to launching, at Harland & Wolff's Belfast yard. *(Richard Faber Collection)*

The *Adriatic* departing on her maiden voyage in May 1907. *(Albert Wilhelmi Collection)*

S.S. ADRIATIC.

and therefore reliable and safe. The overall plan was to build four ships so as to provide weekly sailings from both Liverpool and New York.

Built by White Star's favourite Harland & Wolff yard at Belfast in Northern Ireland, the 21,000grt, 705ft-long *Celtic* was the first of the initial pair to be completed. She was commissioned in the summer of 1901. She too dazzled the interested public with her size, her luxuries and her ability to carry as many as 2,875 passengers in first class, second class and steerage. Her sister, the *Cedric*, followed with a maiden voyage to New York in the winter of 1903. Just slightly larger, the *Cedric* was listed as the 'world's largest liner' for a time.

White Star's plan for a weekly express service led to its famed and very popular 'Big Four', with the final pair being the *Baltic* and *Adriatic*. They were bigger still, at over 24,000 tons each and somewhat longer at 726ft, but carried just about the same number of passengers: 2,875 in three classes. They too had superb first-class quarters, but would earn their greatest profits in lower-deck steerage, with that steady stream of souls seeking new lives – and fortunes – in America. White Star was not content, however, with just the 'Big Four'. Now owned by American tycoon J.P. Morgan but still using the British flag and crews, and therefore thought of as a British-owned company, White Star management now looked to even bigger and longer and more luxurious ships. The company needed to compete and, most of all, keep pace with increasing bigger, faster and more lavish Cunarders that were in the planning and developmental stages.

When White Star was bought-out by J.P. Morgan, the masterful Wall Street financier, the British Government became deeply concerned. Would Britain be losing its place in North Atlantic supremacy?; would there not be big national liners to ferry passengers as well as transport cargo and the all-important mail?; and, in a distant thought, would there not be big liners under the Red Ensign that might be useful in time of war? The Government turned to Cunard. They were still wholly British and so support, especially financial, was arranged to build a pair of 'super-ships': the biggest, fastest Cunarders yet.

Cunard had always been both productive and progressive, and even noteworthy. The 14,100grt sisters *Saxonia* and *Ivernia* had, for example, the largest funnels at sea when they were commissioned in 1900–01; their stacks measured a staggering 106ft from deck level to the cowl top. While the largest passenger ship operator on the Atlantic by 1900, Cunard directors were also keen to compete, enhance profits and popularity, and so were keen to build new tonnage. But many ships in the Cunard fleet were not record-breakers and statistically not notable in any way for even their luxuries and amenities. Many Cunarders were smaller, more work-a-day and created purely for commercial interest. They were used mostly on the North Atlantic, between Liverpool and London to New York, to Boston and to eastern Canada. Cunard also invested in the lucrative westbound migrant trade out of the Mediterranean, mostly from Trieste to New York. The 13,603grt *Carpathia* was a smaller version of the earlier *Ivernia* and *Saxonia*, but an otherwise unnoticed ship. She was used in Mediterranean–New York service, carrying a rather slight 204 in first class and then 1,500 in third class. Built in 1903 at Newcastle, she did find maritime immortality. Outward bound for the Mediterranean (and so quite empty of passengers), she responded to an urgent SOS in the dark morning hours of 15 April 1912. She responded at top speed to the sinking *Titanic* and, while the White Star flagship had already sunk, the little heroic Cunarder eventually rescued 705

Cunard's *Saxonia*, with one of the tallest funnels afloat, departing from the landing stage at Liverpool. *(Richard Faber Collection)*

The famed *Carpathia* outbound in the Hudson River at New York. *(Richard Faber Collection)*

During a Mediterranean cruise, the *Carmania* anchored off Monte Carlo. *(Richard Faber Collection)*

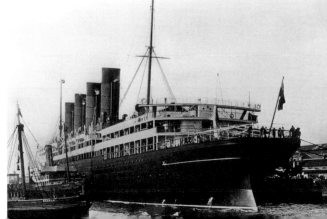

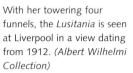

With her towering four funnels, the *Lusitania* is seen at Liverpool in a view dating from 1912. *(Albert Wilhelmi Collection)*

people. Days later, when she reached New York's Pier 54, she was a much-praised ship. These days, within her own maritime immortality and in the brisk memorabilia markets, pieces from her command huge prices because of the direct link to the *Titanic* and her tragedy. Becoming a troopship in the First World War, 558ft-long *Carpathia* was a subsequent casualty, being sunk by a German U-boat off Bishop Rock on 17 July 1918.

Cunard was, however, increasingly troubled by the appearance, in particular, of not only newer and larger liners from White Star, but also from across the North Sea, from Imperial Germany and in the form of the mighty Hamburg America Line and the North German Lloyd. New German liners, it seemed, appeared almost every year. The Hamburg-America Line and the North German Lloyd added the 22,200grt *Amerika* in 1905, then, bigger still, the 24,500grt *Kaisern Auguste Victoria* and, in 1909, the 25,500grt *George Washington*. Cunard responded with two fine liners, neither of which were the world's largest or fastest, but a noted team just the same. They were the *Caronia* and *Carmania*; both commissioned in 1905 and, because of their good looks, were quickly dubbed 'the pretty sisters'. At 19,500 tons each, they carried up to 2,650 passengers – 300 in first class, 350 second class, 900 third class and 1,100 steerage. They were designed especially for the company's Liverpool–New York express service.

But the *Caronia* and *Carmania* were also important test ships. Cunard, while normally conservative and sometimes even cautious, decided to experiment. The new steam-turbine propulsion system was intriguing and some in the maritime industries reported that such drive was the future. The earlier steam quadruple expansion was not especially efficient and was also dirty. So Cunard designers decided to use the older system in the *Caronia* and the newer method on board the *Carmania*. Quickly, the latter proved to be far superior and created faster, more efficient passages. In future, Cunard would use steam turbines on all of its liners. And the next project was Cunard's biggest and grandest yet – building twin super-liners that would be the very fastest on the Atlantic.

The 31,550grt *Lusitania* was the first of the new pair, being commissioned in September 1907. She was a splendid ship, sailing out of the famed John Brown yard on the Clyde and off to her first trials. She was 'crowned' by four enormously tall funnels, each done in the Cunard Company's red-orange and black. While the earlier German four-stackers had grouped their funnels in two pairs (an idea which Cunard did consider), they – more sensibly – balanced the distance between each stack. The effect to many was greater and more appealing to the eye. Funnels were great symbols to the travelling public and emphasised a ship's size as well as its safety. The 787ft-long *Lusitania* had four of the tallest funnels yet to go to sea.

Gloriously, the *Lusitania* reached 25 knots on her trials. She was soon the Blue Riband champion of the Atlantic. Cunard could not have been more pleased and she soon settled down, with her near-sister, *Mauretania*, to a very comfortable and profitable relay on the Liverpool–New York express run.

But if the *Lusitania* was pleasing, the *Mauretania* was pure dreamboat, especially to Cunard and the British nation. She wrested the prized Blue Riband in 1908 and then kept it for an unparalleled twenty-two years. There was no greater distinction or higher prestige. In November 1908, her record run exceeded a staggering 26 knots.

As built, the *Mauretania* could carry 2,335 passengers – 560 first class, 475 second class and 1,300 third class. Predictably, the first-class interiors were nothing short of sea-going magnificence. While the *Lusitania*'s upper-deck quarters ranged from French Renaissance to English country and included the likes of an ornate glass skylight, an Edwardian restaurant and a tree-filled verandah cafe, the *Mauretania* was said to be darker and heavier in decoration. Amidst the splendours of highly polished woods, crystal chandeliers and lamps, and thick, specially made carpets, her decor was appraised as being 'continental' with major French influences and even touches of the Italian Renaissance. She was, being the Riband holder, immensely popular and hugely profitable.

But in the quest for greater size and more sumptuous luxuries and amenities, the Atlantic liner race continued – at full steam ahead! By 1910, White Star was planning a trio of 46–48,000 tonners – the *Olympic*, the *Titanic* and, bigger still, the *Gigantic* (later renamed *Britannic*). But the Hamburg America Line would pull out all the stops with the most colossal ships yet to sail – a successively larger threesome: the 52,000-ton *Imperator*, then the 54,000-ton *Vaterland* and finally the 56,000-ton *Bismarck*.

White Star was still not, from a management perspective, interested in record-breaking speed and therefore avoided the ever-changing contest for the fabled Blue Riband. Instead, the company's goals were in size, luxury and creating the best ships possible. They needed to compete, of course, with Cunard and therefore planned their trio of huge liners. The 45,300-ton *Olympic* came into service in 1911 and seemed to attract the greatest attention, as most first ships of any group and class do. The 46,300-ton *Titanic* followed, but then sank on 15 April, on her maiden crossing to New York no less. It was a horrific disaster, the worst maritime tragedy of its time, and has remained an enduring obsession. Said to be the world's first and only 'unsinkable ship', the tragedy claimed an estimated 1,522 lives, leaving only a mere 705 to survive. Ripped open by an iceberg in the western Atlantic, some 380 miles east of Newfoundland, she went to the bottom, breaking in half in the final plunge, in three hours. Cunard's smallish *Carpathia* arrived too late for a fully effective rescue. Only 32 per cent of all on board the 882ft-long flagship were saved. White Star Line would never again be quite the same, nor would the British shipping trade. Safety standards were changed and increased almost immediately. The *Olympic* was sent quickly to a shipyard, for example, and given additional lifeboats.

Much has been written about the *Titanic* and her tragedy in hundreds of books and thousands of magazine and newspaper articles. She has also been the subject of numerous television documentaries and the star of Hollywood's first billion-dollar film (1997), as well as a Broadway musical. There's even been a specialised Titanic cookbook.

The sinking of a big, unsinkable liner on her maiden voyage has spawned *Titanic* enthusiast and research groups all over the world. There are two in the United States and others in Canada, the UK, France, Germany, Switzerland, Scandinavia, South Africa, Australia and New Zealand. Charles Haas has written five books to date on the *Titanic* and her tragedy and has made two trips, in 1993 and '96, in a submersible down to the wreckage of the White Star liner:

> In all, they were 9-hour journeys, travelling to and from the ship, which rests some 10,000 feet from the open sea. With two crewmen, I travelled in a sphere that was just 7ft wide and likened to a small elevator. It was very small and very close. It was, of

The stately *Mauretania* passing the lower New York skyline in a photograph dated 8 April 1931. *(Richard Faber Collection)*

The *Titanic* in the Belfast Lough. *(Albert Wilhelmi Collection)*

S.S. 'Titanic' - In Belfast Lough - April 1912

course, a life-changing experience to examine the wreckage of a ship that has been a central part of my life for forty years.

Haas added:

But sadly, with the likes of global warming and other changes, the wreck of the *Titanic* will probably be nothing more than rust spots in two places within 50 years. She is now decaying at a much faster rate. During my last visit, there were holes in the decks and the superstructure is collapsing. There was a drastic difference in three years, between my first and second underwater visits. Many others have been down to see the wreckage, including Commodore Ronald Warwick, then master of the biggest Atlantic liner, the *Queen Mary 2*. A couple was even married at the wreck sight, having gone down in separate submersibles and with the minister conducting the service from above from an expedition ship. It cost $40,000 per person.

In April 2012, for the centenary of the sinking, a special *Titanic* remembrance cruise will follow the same westward path of the otherwise ill-fated liner. Reservations were being taken as early as 2005 and since then the *Balmoral*, a Fred Olsen Line cruise ship, has been chartered for the voyage. Charles Haas and other experts will be among the guest speakers. Interest remains high; two years in advance of the sailing, by the winter of 2010, the 1,400-bed ship was all but sold out completely. Also in the winter of 2010, a poster of the *Olympic* and *Titanic* was offered for sale in New York for $36,000.

Earlier, a postcard mailed from the ship at her last port of call at Queenstown fetched $43,000 at auction and a luncheon menu card from her delivery voyage from Belfast to Southampton was bought for $75,000. A ledger of survivor names from the rescue operations at Halifax changed hands for $50,000.

A last link to the survivors of the *Titanic* was severed, in fact, in the autumn of 2009. Milvina Dean, who was a mere nine weeks old when her parents took her on that *Titanic* crossing, died that May at the age of ninety-seven. That November, with some 150 friends and *Titanic* enthusiasts watching, her ashes were scattered from the Southampton Docks, quite close to where the liner had departed.

The *Gigantic* was to be the third of White Star's super-ships; the last of that glorious trio needed to maintain a weekly Southampton–Cherbourg–Queenstown–New York express service. It had the greatest potential and seemed the ideal competition to Cunard's express service and their trio of *Lusitania*, *Mauretania* and, due in 1914, the *Aquitania*. The 48,100-ton *Gigantic* was to be completed by Harland & Wolff's ever-industrious yard at Belfast in 1915. She was the larger of the White Star threesome. Soon after the *Titanic* was lost, however, her name was changed to a more patriotic *Britannic*. But like the *Titanic*, this ship's life was indeed very short. Her construction was halted almost immediately in the late summer of 1914 as the First World War dramatically erupted and engulfed the British merchant fleet in more urgent and pressing concerns. She was finally completed over a year later, in November 1915, but as a hospital ship and for duties in the troubled eastern Mediterranean. She was painted overall in International Red Cross livery and had a staggering 3,300 beds (second only to the *Aquitania*, which

New York City built the 900ft-long Chelsea piers in 1905–07 in preparation for the maiden arrivals of the *Lusitania* and *Mauretania*. Closed by the 1960s, they mostly fell into disrepair by the time this photograph was taken on 1 July 1978. Some of the piers were demolished in the 1990s. *(Richard Faber Collection)*

had 4,182 beds in her role as a hospital ship). Almost pathetically, the new *Britannic* lasted only a year. She was sunk in the Aegean by a German-laid mine on 21 November 1916. Twenty-one aboard were lost, and now, together with the *Titanic*, White Star had lost two of its finest and largest liners. In ways, the company would never again be quite the same.

Other British liner companies serving on the Atlantic had added new tonnage, if far smaller and even less noteworthy, in that first decade of the new century. The Allan Line was a prime entry in the busy UK–Canada passenger service. They reached a zenith by 1905 with their 10,700grt *Virginian* and her sister, the *Victorian*. Built at Glasgow, they were the first Atlantic liners to use steam turbine drive. At a full speed of 18 knots, the 538ft-long *Virginian* also ranked as the fastest liner serving eastern Canada. Her record between Liverpool and Quebec City was an amazing five days and twenty hours. While the *Victorian* finished her days (as the *Marloch* for Canadian Pacific) and went quietly to the breakers in 1929, the 1,712-passenger *Virginian* turned out to be one of the longest lasting Atlantic liners of all time. While transferred to Canadian Pacific Steamships during the First World War, in 1917, she was sold out of the British register to the Swedish American Line in 1920. She sailed as their *Drottningholm* until 1948 and then became the *Brasil* for the then newly formed Home Lines, a multinational firm using the Panamanian flag, before changing to *Homeland* in 1951. With a career spanning fifty years and as a testament to great British shipbuilding, she was finally sold for scrap in 1955.

Another company specialising in the Canadian Atlantic service was Montreal-based Canadian Pacific, which owned the largest transportation system anywhere in the world and included ships, rails and road transportation. Their London-headquartered shipping division grew steadily and was capped, by 1906, by their largest liners yet, the 15,600-ton *Empress of Britain* and *Empress of Ireland*. They sailed for about half the year, when the St Lawrence River was ice-free and open, between Liverpool and Quebec City; for the remainder, their crossings terminated at St John, New Brunswick. While the *Empress of Britain* went on to sail for twenty-four years (and later as the *Montroyal*), the *Empress of Ireland* had far more notoriety. On 29 May 1914, while in thick fog in the St Lawrence, she was rammed by a Norwegian freighter. Mortally wounded, the 570ft-long *Empress* sank within minutes and claimed 1,024 lives. Coming just two years after the *Titanic*'s loss (with an estimated 1,522 casualties), the loss of the *Empress* was the second worst tragedy in the annals of British shipping. Then more great tragedy: a year later, the *Lusitania* was torpedoed with 1,198 lost. Combined, some 3,600 souls perished within three years and all on British liners.

In the wake of the *Mauretania* and *Lusitania*, and as increased competition to the White Star Line and their giant ships, Cunard built a third super-liner. Launched in April 1913 at the John Brown yard at Clydebank, she had one of the most perfect names for a ship, especially a big, luxurious, romantic liner. The *Aquitania* was named for the Roman province that became south-west France. Cunard had never used the name before, but it seemed an ideal choice for their newest, largest, most palatial luxury vessel of that high-spirited era just before the sinister onslaught of the First World War. The 45,647grt ship was commissioned in May 1914, but she was barely in service when the 'war to end all wars' dramatically erupted that August. The 901ft-long *Aquitania* was promptly turned over to the British Government for far less luxurious, but more urgent duties trooping and, later, service as a huge floating hospital.

The Carolean smoking room aboard the very popular *Aquitania*. *(Albert Wilhelmi Collection)*

The North Atlantic route, between the Old World and the New, that week-long passage or so between continents, was at its peak just before the hostilities began in earnest. Alone, 1 million immigrants crossed in third class and steerage, the most lucrative, profit-making and therefore desirous of trades to the likes of Cunard directors. Upper-deck first-class and second-class quarters were filled with the travellers, the tourists, those trans-ocean commuters – the merchants, the teachers and students, and those on summer holidays, and of course that steady flow of the rich and titled, the tycoons and the royalties. For this, the 23-knot *Aquitania* catered beautifully. Her accommodations in first class were almost dream-like, a fantasy world gone to sea. To some there were no finer public rooms, lounges and salons afloat than her Carolean smoking room, her Palladian lounge and her Louis XVI restaurant. There was also an Adam drawing room, a Jacobean grill room and an indoor 'swimming bath' decorated with replicas of Egyptian ornaments held in the British Museum in London. The late ocean liner historian and author John Malcolm-Brinnin wrote of her, 'The *Aquitania* was the last word and ultimate extension of a kind of interior decoration reflecting a way of life on which World War I would draw a curtain. If acquisitions defined wealth and power then the *Aquitania* was a ship of acquisitions.' The handsomely proportioned, four-funnel *Aquitania* was also said to be, by many, the most beautiful ship of all the seas. In fact, she was soon dubbed 'the Ship Beautiful'.

Away from the Atlantic and in those years just prior to the First World War, British shipowners were also building bigger, often faster and usually more comfortable if not luxurious passenger ships. Britain was the commercial trading power of the world. Her factories produced the goods that were sent to the farthest corners of the earth and all while the country itself needed a vast array of goods in return. And then, of course, there was the still quite extraordinary empire and where it remained 'that the sun never set'.

In May 1911, at the coronation of George V and Queen Mary in London, hundreds of thousands attended. Every corner of the globe was represented, it seemed, and all the overseas guests and visitors and spectators came by sea, often in British passenger vessels. There were Americans that travelled Cunard or White Star; Argentines that used Royal Mail Lines; Sikhs and Gurkhas that came on P&O; Hausas from West Africa that sailed in Elder Dempster Line ships; and even Frenchmen from Canada that sailed across on Canadian Pacific. It was the age of vast maritime connections and Britain's liner fleet was the largest and most extensive on earth. Every continent, or so it appeared, was connected to London, Liverpool, Glasgow or Southampton.

Royal Mail Lines was the dominant firm on the UK-east coast of South America trade by the turn of the century. They competed with other British shipping lines as well as the French and Germans, but were noted for the finest passenger ships of their day. The company's mainline service from Southampton, via Vigo, Lisbon and Las Palmas, to Rio de Janeiro, Santos, Montevideo and Buenos Aires was strengthened by the introduction, beginning in 1906, of a succession of new liners. They began with the 10,000-ton *Amazon* and then, each slightly larger, the *Araguaya*, *Avon* and *Asturias*. Then, by 1911, they added four more ships, each also successively larger. These began with the 15,000-ton *Arlanza*, completed in 1912, followed by the *Andes*, *Alcantara* and finally the *Almanzora*. The 589ft-long *Andes* would be the longest lasting of them, becoming the highly popular cruise ship *Atlantis* in 1930 and not being retired and scrapped until

Headlines from *The New York Times* dated 16 April 1912. *(Author's Collection)*

1952. Furthermore, and as British shipping was booming, Royal Mail added no less than five more liners – the 11,500grt *Deseado*, *Demerara*, *Desna*, *Darro* and *Drina* – to its fleet in 1911–12.

Liverpool-based Lamport & Holt Line was also deeply interested in Latin American service, but from New York down along the east coast of South America as well. Beginning in 1909, they added a series of 10,000-tonners, large passenger and cargo

The launch of the mighty *Britannic* at Belfast on 26 February 1914. *(Albert Wilhelmi Collection)*

vessels that each carried almost 600 passengers in three classes, named *Vasari*, *Vandyck*, *Vauban* and *Vestris*. The Belfast-built *Vestris* would later make her mark in the annals of passenger ship disasters. On a voyage to Brazil in November 1928, she was just two days out of New York when the 511ft-long ship ran into heavy weather and, as her cargo and bunkers shifted, she developed a severe list. An SOS was sent out but she sank soon thereafter with the loss of 112 of the 325 on board.

Alternately, to the west coast of South America to ports such as Guayaquil, Callao and Valparaiso, the Pacific Steamship Navigation Co. had great interests. Sailing from Liverpool on extended voyages across to the Caribbean and through the then new Panama Canal were, among others, five new steamers – the *Orduna*, *Orbita*, *Orca*, *Oropresa* and *Oroya*. The last three were, in fact, delayed by the approaching First World War and commissioned between 1918–23.

In 1900, two British companies, the Union Steam Collier Company and Castle Mail Packets Company, sensibly merged to create the Union-Castle Mail Steamship Company Limited, which would become the mightiest shipping line in the African trades to and from the UK. They were supported by lucrative Government mail contracts as well as a steady flow of passengers, and so it began building successively larger, finer and faster passenger ships. One of six new sisters, the 13,326grt, 16-knot *Edinburgh Castle* could make the express run (from Southampton, and with a short stop at either Las Palmas or Madeira, to Cape Town) in sixteen days. Afterwards, the 810-passenger vessel would continue on to Port Elizabeth, East London and then turn around at Durban.

Out to the East, beyond Suez to India, the Far East as well as Australia and New Zealand, London-based Peninsular & Oriental Steam Navigation Co. Ltd dominated. Quite simply, they were known as 'the P&O' and were, according to no less than Rudyard Kipling, 'the most vital link of the empire'. Their ships were poetically described as being 'on long, tropical voyages, with curry lunches and long afternoon naps and sailing the Eastern seas under charcoal-coloured, star-filled nights'. High commissioners and occasional royal potentates, rich tea planters and seemingly endless armies of civil servants of the crown filled their decks, lounges and staterooms. On the long but important seven-week run between London, Melbourne and Sydney via Suez, P&O added a new trio – the *Morea*, *Malwa* and *Mantua* – in 1908. Carrying considerable cargo and lots of mail, they had passenger quarters for 407 in first class and 200 in second class.

Externally, they were typically unique P&O ships, being painted in with black hulls and dark upper-works, commonly referred to as 'stone colour'.

P&O's Australian service only prospered further; by 1910, as the likes of the *Olympic* and *Titanic* were in the works, new and larger ships were ordered for Eastern services. These included the 12,300grt *Maloja* and *Medina*. The 625ft-long *Maloja*, introduced in September 1911, had a rather unique maiden voyage: a cruise from London up to the Hebrides and back. P&O was, of course, the originator of pleasure cruising, begun in the late 1840s. But the *Medina* had an even greater distinction. For her commissioning

The splendid *Aquitania* outbound at New York with the Statue of Liberty in the background. *(Richard Faber Collection)*

A First World War casualty: Cunard's 18,100-ton *Franconia* sinking in the Mediterranean on 4 October 1916. *(Richard Faber Collection)*

in October 1911, she was chartered to the Royal Navy for a very special role – serving as a Royal Yacht. She was fitted out with a white hull, given a specially added third mast and her first-class passenger accommodations were restyled with furnishings from the royal collection, mostly from the royal yacht *Victoria and Albert*. That November, with great fanfare, she set off from Portsmouth with King George V and Queen Mary and their entourage on board. They were bound for Bombay, for the Delhi Durbar. A highly successful visit in terms of empire-building, the King and Queen returned seven months later, again on the *Medina*. There might have been some added concern on this homeward voyage. It was only weeks since the *Titanic* had been tragically lost in the western Atlantic.

P&O was also interested in the expanding and therefore profitable migrant trade to Australia and, between 1911 and 1913, added five 11,100grt sister ships, the *Ballarat*, *Beltana*, *Benalla*, *Berrima* and *Borda*. They were the most basic of ships, however, each carrying five holds of cargo and 1,100 third-class passengers.

The primary rival to P&O on the long-haul but very important and profitable UK–Australian run was another London-based company, the Orient Line. This firm was especially noted for its very fine first-class quarters and excellent food and service. They used an 'O' nomenclature and so, when adding no less than six fast liners for the London–Sydney service, they were named *Orsova*, *Otway*, *Osterley*, *Otranto*, *Orvieto* and *Orama*. Being 18-knot ships and carrying up nearly 1,100 passengers (in three classes), they offered a prized amenity to passengers: a sailing every fortnight from London as well as Sydney.

Blue Funnel Line, based in Liverpool, had vast interests in both the Australian and Far Eastern trades. By 1910 their growing fleet was enhanced with their largest ships yet, great passenger-cargo vessels with noticeably tall, blue-coloured funnels. The 10,000-ton

Aeneas and her sisters, the *Ascanius* and *Anchises*, carried as many as 288 first-class passengers each on the UK–Australia run. Alternatively, there was the similar-sized *Talthybius* and *Ixion*, which carried 600 but only in austere steerage. The first-class Australian trade warranted further tonnage, however, and in 1912 included the addition of the 14,500grt *Nestor* and *Ulysses*, which catered for up to 350 passengers each.

While largely remembered for its North Atlantic liner services, the famed White Star Line also invested in the Australian trade. They preferred, however, to use the longer route from the UK via South Africa and concentrated almost entirely on the low-fare migrant trade. Alone, in the two years between 1911 and 1913, some 200,000 Britons migrated to Australia and New Zealand. In 1913, White Star added the 18,481grt *Ceramic* for their service between Liverpool and Sydney via Cape town. A large vessel at 679ft in length and capped by one large funnel and four masts, she carried 600 third-class passengers only. Distinctive as the largest ship on the Australian run, she was dubbed the 'Queen of the Southern Ocean' and later sailed for another British liner firm, Shaw Savill, until tragically lost in the Second World War in December 1942. She was torpedoed west of the Azores by a German U-boat, sinking within minutes and all but one of the 656 on board perished.

Canadian Pacific, which used British registry for its large liners, reinforced its dominance on the trans-Pacific route between Vancouver and the Far East with two significant liners, the 16,900grt *Empress of Russia* and *Empress of Asia*. Three-stackers, and therein resembling something of the great Atlantic liners, they were notable ships – the largest, fastest and finest then in Pacific service. Aboard the 592ft-long, 20-knot *Empress of Russia* there was accommodation for 284 in first class, 100 in second class and 808 in Asiatic steerage, and all looked after by a crew of 475.

The First World War wreaked havoc on the British passenger ship fleet. Commercial

Another Cunarder lost: specially converted to an aircraft carrier, the 12,900grt *Campania* sinking in the Firth of Forth in November 1918. *(Richard Faber Collection)*

The big troopship *Justicia*, intended to be the Holland America liner *Statendam* but seized by the British Government and then operated by White Star, sinking off the Irish coast in July 1918. *(Richard Faber Collection)*

services were halted and often abruptly, ships repainted in sombre greys and stripped of their fineries, and then – worst of all – many were destroyed. Many would be sunk by sinister German U-boats. Almost a third of the British merchant fleet was gone by the time of the Armistice in November 1918.

Many liners were sensibly converted to troopships, while others became hospital ships and armed merchant cruisers. Cunard's *Carmania*, a 19,500-ton liner, was quickly made over as an armed merchant cruiser and made news early in the war. On 14 September, off Trinidad, she engaged the German liner *Cap Trafalgar*. Numerous shots were fired from the guns mounted on the Cunarder and the 18,800-ton Hamburg-South America liner soon sank. While damaged and with many shell holes, the *Carmania* made for port and was later repaired. Later, for Christmas 1918, she was back in Cunard's Atlantic service.

Big liners, such as the *Olympic*, had a heroic record by war's end. For example, by 1918 the *Olympic* had been proudly and lovingly dubbed 'Old Reliable'. Early on in the hostilities, in October 1914, she attempted to tow the badly damaged battleship HMS *Audacious* to safety in the River Clyde. Although the warship later sank, the troopship *Olympic* rescued the entire crew. She had close calls too, mostly from U-boat attacks later in the war, but finished with a record of safely delivering 200,000 troops. White Star, like Cunard, was proud of their wartime record by the Armistice of November 1918. White Star ships had carried 525,000 troops and over 4 million tons of cargo.

The worst tragedy of the war was the sinking of Cunard's giant *Lusitania*. She was mercilessly torpedoed while acting as a commercial liner when sailing off the south-eastern coast of Ireland in May 1915. Badly damaged, listing and sinking by

the bow, she slipped under the waters of the Irish Sea not far from Queenstown. Of the 1,959 passengers and crew on board, 1,198 perished including 128 still-neutral American passengers. In the aftermath, the loss of the *Lusitania* helped lure the United States into the war against Germany.

Altogether, Britain's merchant navy suffered during that 'war to end all wars'. Over 6 million tons, or 30 per cent, of the nation's ships were sunk and, specifically among these, Cunard lost thirty of its ships, including the aforementioned *Lusitania*, as well as the far smaller but heroic *Carpathia*, famous from the *Titanic* disaster. Everyone, it seems, joined in the cause. Cunard managed no less than 500 ships during the war and, separate from shipping in 1915, ran a factory that produced 500,000 cannon shells. Two years later, Cunard was also managing the biggest aircraft factory in Britain.

The end of the First World War brought about considerable change to the British passenger ship industry. Alone, countless ships needed to be restored and rebuilt, many others needed to be replaced and then there were ships brought over to the Red Ensign as reparations. Biggest of these, the 56,500grt *Bismarck*, confiscated from the defeated Germans, was allocated to White Star, becoming their flagship and the largest liner afloat, renamed the *Majestic*. Cunard was given her slightly smaller near-sister, the former *Imperator*, which changed to *Berengaria*. In due course, in the early 1920s, and because of lingering ill-will and resentment towards the wartime enemy, White Star and Cunard worked hard at erasing the most evident German touches aboard these big liners.

two

RESUMPTION & RESTORATION: POST-FIRST WORLD WAR

High honour! Their Majesties King George V and Queen Mary visited the *Majestic*, the new flagship of White Star and the largest ship on all the seas, in August 1922. The royal couple tendered out in the Solent as the flag-bedecked liner waited, ready for her maiden crossing to New York. Sparkling in fresh paint and flying the royal standards from her towering mast and seeming enormous as she sat at anchor, the *Majestic* would become a great success, carrying 2,625 passengers on a 1925 crossing, and the highest for any ship of that time. Popular with trans-ocean travellers of the 1920s, the *Majestic* was also well known in the United States as a very popular sight in New York harbour and was affectionately dubbed 'the Magic Stick'. Like other British liners, she was also a great floating ambassador: she showed the flag.

Recovery was the theme in the British liner trades in the early 1920s. There were also some changes to be reckoned with; namely the immigration quotas created by the American government which cut deeply into the fast profits of third-class travel on British passenger ships heading mostly for New York. A new tourist class, or at least an improved third class, had to be created in place of austere steerage and the third-class standards of pre-1914. Fortunately, a new wave of tourist-class travellers, somewhat restricted by wallets and budgets, would emerge and were more than happy to fill lower-deck berths.

Alone, Cunard had lost eleven passenger ships during the war and as peace returned more and more berths were needed. The company was hard pressed at times and chartered a diverse group of passenger ships, some for only one or two voyages. They looked to Union-Castle, Pacific Steam Navigation and Lamport & Holt. They even chartered P&O's *Kaisar-i-Hind*, normally on the London–Bombay route, but sensibly advertised it to the Atlantic travelling public as the translated *Emperor of India*.

There was no immediate interest in building big new ships in the early 1920s. Cunard and White Star made do, as you might say. The former had the *Mauretania*, *Aquitania* and the newly acquired ex-German *Berengaria* under its house-flag, while White Star had the *Olympic*, *Majestic* (also ex-German) and the *Homeric*, which was the intended German *Columbus*, but never completed as such. The grand age of the four-stacker – those Edwardian floating palaces – was, of course, over. A new, more modern, sleeker age was ahead. Instead, from its traditional and always cautious Liverpool headquarters, Cunard looked in the 1920s to more moderate tonnage, groups of passenger ships of 15–20,000

tons. White Star, falling on increasingly hard times, built far fewer ships, though this included the twin-funnel *Laurentic* in 1927, the last coal-burner in the British merchant fleet.

The *Aquitania* was among the greatest liners to survive the First World War intact. Those grey troopship colours were chipped away by early 1919, in that first year of peace. She was soon back in her Cunard finery – a long, black hull, snow-white upper-works and that quartet of lofty funnels capped by black tops and then coloured in Cunard's distinctive orange-red, created in a supposed historic blend of buttermilk and ochre. Having just the right balance and rake, she looked splendid, every inch the grand ocean liner. The finishing touch was her graceful counter and overhanging stern. But she was back in the shipyard from November 1919 and then through the following summer for major surgery. Progress had taken an aggressive hold and so, like just about all liners, she was converted from coal-burning to oil-fired engines. She was now more efficient, more profitable and below decks those notorious 200 or so stokers, the 'black gangs' as they were called, were gone in a snap. Hereafter, and shifted from the Cunard main terminal at Liverpool to Southampton, the *Aquitania* worked in tandem as part of Cunard's 'Big Three', the trio of express liners that sailed weekly between Southampton, Cherbourg and New York. The other two were the still-speedy, highly popular *Mauretania* and Cunard's flagship, the former *Imperator*, now sailing as the *Berengaria*.

The *Aquitania* – which had a passenger capacity of 2,200 by the mid-1920s, divided as 610 first class, 950 second class and 640 tourist class – was immensely successful at that time. Evidently, her reputation went beyond her splendid decor but was also based on service and was said by some Atlantic sea travellers to be the very best afloat. Generally, all Cunarders enjoyed enviable accolades for their service to guests. 'The *Aquitania* had the advantage,' wrote John Malcolm Brinnin, 'of a crew trained in a sort of father-to-son heritage of stewardship that marked whole families in Liverpool and Southampton. They gave service on a scale of British tact, grace and professionalism that positively dazzled American travellers.'

The *Aquitania* was also very popular with budgeted, often young, usually spirited travellers who crossed in 'tourist third class', reworked from the largely abolished pre-war steerage. (US government immigration restrictions had cut deeply into that profitable flow of westbound humanity in 1924. The million or so migrants that sailed westward in 1914 had disintegrated to a mere 150,000 a decade later.) 'On the lower decks of

The world's largest liner between 1922 and 1935, the 56,500grt *Majestic* is outbound at New York, passing the Woolworth Building (*centre*) and the Singer Building (*right*). (*Albert Wilhemi Collection*)

Grand opening of the King George V Graving Dock at Southampton in 1934. Dressed in flags, the 956ft-long *Majestic* is the first to use the facility. (*Albert Wilhelmi Collection*)

An aerial view of the arriving *Berengaria* in the Ocean Dock at Southampton. White Star's *Homeric* is berthed on the right. (*Frank O. Braynard Collection*)

The first class main lounge on board the popular *Berengaria*. (*Albert Wilhelmi Collection*)

ships like the *Aquitania* were now students, teachers, artists, the tourists,' noted Brinnin. 'Suddenly, in the 1920s, overseas travel lost its character as an adventure fraught with hazards and became an extended outing under the leadership, perhaps, of a professional guide from Atlanta or Minneapolis and, in any case, watched over by American Express.'

Even larger and the official flagship of the very prestigious Cunard Line, the *Berengaria* was equally as popular. One American tycoon so loved her that he booked his favourite suite on board for ten years. In another case, a first-class lady reported that her dog was indulged and spoilt more on board the *Berengaria* than any of the other big liners then on the Atlantic. Despite her German construction and heritage, she ranked, because of her 52,200 tons and 919ft in length, as the flagship of the entire Cunard fleet. In contrast, when she was offering reduced cheap cruises in the Depression-era 1930s, she was nicknamed the 'Bargain-area'.

Cunard did embark on a very ambitious rebuilding programme, one that included no less than fourteen new passenger ships in all. There was one 'misfit' in the group, however, the odd duck *Albania* of 1920. Half passenger and half freighter, she did not seem to fit into Cunard's schedules and so was withdrawn within five years, laid-up for five years and then sold to Italian buyers. Otherwise, Cunard looked to more 'intermediate' liners, beginning with three identical sisters – the 19,700grt *Scythia* of 1920 and then the *Samaria* and *Laconia*. They were dominated by rather tall single funnels and were ships that could be used on the New York or Canadian runs or, on occasion, for winter cruising. The 624ft-long *Laconia* offered the very first around-the-world cruise from New York in 1922, for example.

Two modified sisters followed, the *Franconia* and *Carinthia*, completed in 1923 and 1925 respectively. They were noteworthy in being among the world's first dual-purpose liners. On the Atlantic run, mostly between Liverpool and New York, they could carry three classes of passengers, including a large number of westbound immigrants in lower-deck third class. But alternately, and mostly during the slow winter months, they could be converted, and quite easily, for about 400 first-class passengers only and sent off on luxurious, warm-weather cruises. More specifically, they were used for some of Cunard's first around-the-world cruises. Some of these trips lasted for as long as 180 days, leaving New York in late December and returning in June. As another example, in January 1937, the *Franconia*'s world cruise was advertised as travelling the equivalent of one and a half times around the world. In 144 days, she would travel over 35,000 miles. Outbound from New York, the general itinerary included Trinidad, Brazil, St Helena, Cape Town and Durban in South Africa, Madagascar, the Seychelles, India, Ceylon, the so-called Straits Settlements, Malaya, Siam, Java, Bali, the Philippine Islands, China, Korea, Japan, the Hawaiian Islands, California and Panama. Passage fares, which included some shore-side excursions, started at $1,900.

The *Franconia* and *Carinthia* were later repainted from their North Atlantic black hull colouring to a more tropical, heat-resistant white. They were also refitted on several occasions in Cunard's effort to improve standards and be more competitive in the long cruise business. Amenities on board the *Franconia* included a two-deck-high smoking room done in the style of the fifteenth-century residence of El Greco, twin garden lounges complete with ferns and potted palms, an indoor pool, a racquetball court and even a chocolate shop.

R·M·S· CARINTHIA
ON WORLD CRUISE
AT CIRCULAR QUAY
SYDNEY. N.S.W.
26/2/33.

At the same time, Cunard also bought the *Tyrrhenia* from the Anchor Line, but soon rechristened her as the *Lancastria*. Afterwards, they reworked the design of the earlier 20,000-ton *Scythia* class into six slightly smaller sister ships of 14,000 tons: the *Antonia*, *Ausonia*, *Andania*, *Aurania*, *Ascania* and *Alaunia*.

By comparison, White Star built only two new passenger ships in the early and mid-1920s. The 16,500grt *Doric* was added in 1922 and then, slightly larger, the 18,700grt *Laurentic* in 1927. The *Doric* went on to be one of the saddest victims of the Depression of the 1930s. After a collision in September 1935, the thirteen-year-old liner was sold, without reluctance, for scrapping rather than repairs. But even more tragic was the case of the twin sisters *Minnewaska* and *Minnetonka*, large combination passenger-cargo ships, but carrying only 369 first-class passengers on the London–New York, which were complete failures. Owned by the Atlantic Transport Line, these 22,000grt sisters were sold to ship-breakers in 1933–34 when they were just a decade old.

Glasgow's Anchor Line reinforced its North Atlantic operations to New York between 1921 and 1923 with a series of new ships: four single-stackers, the 16,200-grt *Cameronia* and *Tyrrhenia*, and then, slightly larger, the 16,900grt *Tuscania* and *California*. These were soon followed, in 1925, by a pair of mightier-looking triple-stackers, the 16,900grt sisters *Transylvania* and *Caledonia*. Glasgow based as well, the Donaldson Line added its largest passenger ships ever, the 13,400grt sisters *Athenia* and *Letitia*, in 1923 and 1925 respectively. They were designed for the Canadian Atlantic run, trading between Glasgow and Montreal. Afterwards, in 1928–29, Canadian Pacific became more competitive in its Atlantic liner operations when they added four smart-looking, well-decorated 20,100-tonners, the *Duchess of Atholl*, *Duchess of Bedford*, *Duchess of Richmond* and *Duchess of York*. Built by John Brown yard on the Clyde, they were preludes to the giant *Empress of Britain*, a 42,000-tonner that would emerge several years later in 1931.

Soon after the traumatic Wall Street Crash in October 1929, even much-loved ships such as Cunard's *Aquitania* began to fall on hard times. The Atlantic trade slid steadily and almost hopelessly into decline; the 1 million passengers of, say, 1930 plummeted to half that number within five years. Cunard, like all ship owners, was worried, in fact very worried. And to complicate matters even further, the company had just reviewed the plans of the *Aquitania*, then revised and extended them, changed the decorative theme to the new Art Deco style and ordered a mammoth ship of at least 79,000 tons. She would become the illustrious *Queen Mary*, commissioned in 1936.

Left, from top

The *Berengaria* passes a line of battleships assembled for King George V's Jubilee Naval Review at Southampton in May 1935. *(Albert Wilhelmi Collection)*

The *Carinthia* during a world cruise, berthed at Sydney. This view is dated 26 February 1933. *(Albert Wilhelmi Collection)*

A dramatic aerial view of the Southampton Docks in 1933. The *Alcantara* and *Strathnaver* are in the lower right; the *Olympic*, *Aquitania*, *Berengaria* and *Orontes* are in their Ocean Dock; the *Arandora Star* is just below the stern of the *Olympic*; and the *Mauretania* and *Empress of Britain* are in the upper left. *(Albert Wilhelmi Collection)*

three

FLYING THE RED ENSIGN: SERVING THE EMPIRE

The P&O express train from London, crossing the Channel and then direct to Marseilles, made a special – if short – stop in Paris. The purpose was to collect two very important passengers, their accompanying entourage and, of course, baggage. The Duke and Duchess of York, the future King George VI and Queen Elizabeth (later Queen Elizabeth the Queen Mother) were heading off on an official tour of East Africa. It was decided that they would avoid the often notorious passage through the Bay of Biscay and instead board the *Mulbera*, an otherwise smallish 9,100-tonner owned by the British India Steam Navigation Co. Ltd. This passenger-cargo vessel, with space for 158 passengers, would carry the royal couple and their party across the Mediterranean, through the Suez Canal and to a call at colonial Aden before continuing to another colonial outpost, Mombasa in Kenya. The duchess wrote in her letters and journal: 'Shipboard rituals continued throughout the voyage, including a fancy dress ball [and the duchess in red Spanish shawl and floppy hat] as the judge and the customary Crossing-the-Line ceremony.' Later, at Mombasa, the duchess recorded: 'We were greeted on the quayside by the Governor General, large numbers of people from the British colony, as well as Kenyans, Somalis, Indians and Arabs, all whom helped to cheer us ashore.'

Four months later, in April, they concluded their African visit and boarded P&O's *Maloja* at Port Sudan. While the ship was homeward bound from Australia for London, the duke and duchess again decided on Marseilles, where they disembarked and then got the train to the capital city. 'This was the least enjoyable part of the trip. The sense of the real world was before us,' wrote the duchess.

Britain's trading links with great parts of the world were strengthened in the 1920s with new ships, many of them carrying passengers and mostly improvements over prior tonnage and often faster and thereby cutting voyage times. The business trade of transporting merchants and traders, bankers and technicians was all important.

Royal Mail Lines all but dominated the British trade to the east coast of South America – to Rio de Janeiro, Santos, Montevideo and Buenos Aires – and business looked promising. Beginning in the winter of 1926, they added the sleek squat-funnel pair of *Asturias* and *Alcantara*. Royal Mail directors and designers decided to experiment with a new form of propulsion just coming into vogue. They surpassed the 17,000-ton Swedish American liner *Gripsholm*, commissioned in 1925, as the largest and most powerful motor-liners afloat when they were completed. But their Danish-constructed Burmeister

& Wain diesels proved inadequate in due course and both ships had to be re-fitted with engines eight years later, in 1934, using classic steam turbines. Their service speeds were increased from 16 to 18 knots.

First class (for 410 passengers aboard the 22,071grt *Asturias*) was especially palatial, catering to grand travellers, aristocrats and rich businessmen. Her public rooms were lavish, being done in rich British and empire styles, and included a two-deck-high dining room that could seat all first-class guests at one time. There was also a Moorish-style smoking room, a panelled library and a 29ft-long, tiled indoor pool.

Also running to the East Coast was the Nelson Line, which added no less than six motor-liners beginning in late 1928. They too used the low, flat, squat-funnel design and had 'broken' superstructures with bridge and officer quarters separated by a cargo hold from the passenger accommodations. They were named *Highland Monarch*, *Highland Chieftain*, *Highland Brigade*, *Highland Hope*, *Highland Princess* and finally, completed in May 1932, the *Highland Patriot*. Nelson fell on hard times, however, in the Depression and by 1932 was absorbed into the larger, more secure Royal Mail Lines fleet. Several of the *Highland* ships would serve Royal Mail until as late as 1960.

While primarily interested in the lucrative meat trades homeward to the UK, but also keen on first-class travel to and from the east coast of South America, London's Blue Star Line built five new ships, all intimate combination passenger-cargo ships, beginning in 1926. Often later altered and modified, they were the *Almeda* (soon changed to *Almeda Star*), *Andalucia* (*Andalucia Star*), *Avila* (*Avila Star*), *Avelona* (*Avelona Star*) and finally the *Arandora* (*Arandora Star*). While the *Avelona Star* was later rebuilt as a freighter, the 12,900grt *Arandora Star* went on, beginning in the early 1930s, to become one of Britain's most popular cruise ships.

Away from home ports, the Furness-Prince Line built a quartet of smart combination passenger-cargo ships, the 10,900grt, 100-berth *Northern Prince*, *Eastern Prince*, *Southern Prince* and *Western Prince*, for the New York–Rio–Buenos Aires services. Also in the early 1920s, Lamport & Holt Line, strongly interested in the New York–South America run, added the *Vandyck* and *Voltaire* – two fine 13,200-tonners. And another arm of the Furness Withy shipping empire, the Furness-Bermuda Line, was realising more and more the success of its New York-based service to and from Bermuda. They created the very fine but later ill-fated *Bermuda* in 1927.

Right
With her squat funnels, the 657ft-long *Winchester Castle* was rebuilt in 1938 with a large single funnel. *(Cronican-Arroyo Collection)*

Below
The four-funnel *Windsor Castle* departing from the VIctoria Basin at Cape Town in a scene dated 1925. *(Albert Wilhelmi Collection)*

The first-class music room aboard the *Narkunda*. *(P&O)*

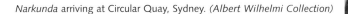

Narkunda arriving at Circular Quay, Sydney. *(Albert Wilhelmi Collection)*

With the flag-bedecked *Orontes* passing below, the opening of the Sydney Harbour Bridge in 1932. *(P&O)*

Dog-racing passengers on a cruise aboard the famed *Viceroy of India* in 1935. *(P&O)*

Union-Castle greatly strengthened its premier Southampton–Cape express run with the delivery of the 661ft–long *Arundel Castle* and *Windsor Castle* – the last four-funnel liners to be built. Designed before the First World War, their completion was delayed until 1921 and '22 respectively. Popular ships for a time, they were rebuilt and modernised with a more contemporary look of twin funnels and raked bows in 1937. (After that, Cunard's *Aquitania* was the last four-stacker on the seas.) They were soon followed by more modern ships in the large Union-Castle fleet, the splendid, squat-funnel motor-liners *Carnarvon Castle*, *Winchester Castle* and *Warwick Castle*. Each at over 20,000 tons, they were for a time the crack ships on the Southampton–Cape Town express run.

The Ellerman Lines, noted for its vast cargo ship fleet, invested in the UK–South Africa as well as the UK–India trades with, among other passenger-cargo types, the likes of the 330-passenger *City of Paris* and the similar *City of Nagpur*.

The ever-evocative P&O was riding a high wave of renewal and rebuilding in the 1920s. The colonial trades were as strong and secure as ever, supplemented by lucrative mail and cargo contracts and the outbound migrant trade down to Australia and New Zealand was brisk. They added the three-funnel sisters *Naldera* and *Narkunda* which had been designed and were actually under construction as the First World War erupted. Delayed, they were not introduced, on the London–Bombay and later on the London–Sydney services, until 1920. To strengthen their colonial Bombay service, P&O added the 16,200grt sisters *Moldavia* and *Mongolia* in 1923. Twin-stackers that carried some 400 passengers each in two classes, the 568ft-long

Mongolia went on to a long career, serving as the *Rimutaka*, *Europa*, *Nassau* and finally the *Acapulco*.

The Belfast-built *Mooltan* and *Maloja*, both commissioned in 1923, were the largest and most luxurious P&O liners to date. At over 20,000 tons and rather unique at the time in having two funnels but only a foremast, they had quarters for comparatively few passengers – 327 in first class and 329 in second class. They were the prime ships for some years on the run from London via Suez to Melbourne and Sydney. Both survived the Second World War and endured (but as low-fare migrant ships) until the early 1950s. Living in Sydney, ship enthusiast Lindsay Johnstone remembered the *Mooltan* and *Maloja* from their final years, in the late 1940s and early '50s. 'They were very, very old world by then. They had very period decor, classic P&O decor from the '20s. Inside, they were like old stately homes with timbered beams and panels, and even had fireplaces. More exactly, they were like a Tudor home, perhaps even a castle in ways.'

P&O further invested in the ever-lucrative Australian migrant business with five 13,000grt ships, commissioned in 1921–22. Named *Ballarat*, *Baradine*, *Balranald*, *Barrabool* and *Bendigo*, they were purposeful and so quite simple, almost austere ships with accommodations for almost 1,200 passengers: 490 in third class and 700 in steerage.

P&O's Indian service was still hugely important and, in the mid-1920s, the company added four 'express ships' – the *Ranpura*, *Ranchi*, *Rawalpindi* and *Rajputana* – for the London–Bombay run. More exactly, these 16,900grt ships were actually routed between London, Marseilles (for train connections to/from London), Malta, Port Said, a transit of

Passengers disembark from the *Maloja* at Marseilles in a photograph from 1948. *(P&O)*

Right, from top
Festive departure: the *Otranto* departing from Sydney for London on 11 March 1950. *(Lindsay Johnstone Collection)*

The *Mongolia* at Barcelona during a cruise in a view from 1933. *(P&O)*

The *Esperance Bay* of the Aberdeen & Commonwealth Line. *(Gillespie-Faber Collection)*

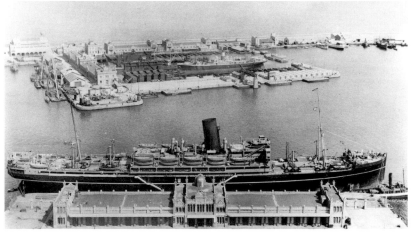

the Suez Canal, Aden and Bombay. The twenty-night voyage from London to Bombay was priced from £60 in first class. A great highlight in the P&O annals as well as British passenger ship history was the creation of the splendid *Viceroy of India* in 1928. She was a larger, much improved version of several earlier P&O ships such as the *Cathay*, *Comorin* and *Chitral*. Launched in September 1928, she was to have been named *Taj Mahal*, but the final selection of *Viceroy of India* seemed more fitting to the trades of empire. Fitted with rather unique turbo-electric engines and able to carry up to 673 passengers in two classes, she also became an immensely popular P&O cruise ship, running summertime trips up to the Norwegian fjords and northern cities and southward to the Canaries and the Mediterranean. Her first-class quarters were said to be splendid, some so comfortable that it was as if passengers never left their London club or home in the English countryside.

Arch-rival to P&O, the Orient Line, added no less than five 20,000-tonners for their London–Sydney service. These ships, following the company's typical 'O' nomenclature, were named *Orama*, *Oronsay*, *Otranto*, *Orford* and *Orontes*.

The twin-funnel *Rangitata* in the Pedro Miguel Locks of the Panama Canal. (*Albert Wilhelmi Collection*)

The *Empress of Canada* sailed in regular service between Vancouver, Victoria and the Far East from 1922 until the outbreak of the Second World War in 1939. (*Cronican-Arroyo Collection*)

The *Empress of Australia* berthed at Southampton with the far larger *Empress of Britain* to the left. This view dates from May 1939. (*Richard Faber Collection*)

The first-class smoking room, done in Louis XIV style, aboard the *Empress of Australia*. (*Cronican-Arroyo Collection*)

Even the Australian government dabbled in the migrant trade by building, between 1921 and 1923, no less than five 13,850grt migrant ships – the *Moreton Bay*, *Largs Bay*, *Hobsons Bay*, *Esperance Bay* and *Jervis Bay*. Unsuccessful, however, they were sold to the White Star Line by 1928, hoisted the British flag and then, by 1933, transferred to the London-based Aberdeen & Commonwealth Line.

Another London-headquartered shipping company, the New Zealand Shipping Co. Ltd, ran an extensive service between London, Curacao, the Panama Canal and then down to Auckland and Wellington. They reinforced this with a trio of new ships, the 16,700grt *Rangitiki*, *Rangitata* and *Rangitane*, in the late 1920s. Each carried up to 600 passengers in two classes but, and quite typically, also carried lots of cargo (British manufactured goods outbound and large consignments of meat and wool on the homeward leg). These ships were actually designed in the mid-1920s with single stacks but were delayed somewhat in construction and then redesigned with twin funnels to give the impression of greater size to the travelling public.

The Bibby Line of Liverpool had strong interests in the trade to colonial Burma. They were also quite conservative. Beginning as late as 1926 and continuing well into the 1930s, they built a series of passenger-cargo ships with four masts. Carrying just under 300 one-class passengers each, there was the *Shropshire*, *Cheshire*, *Staffordshire* and *Worcestershire*. A fifth ship, the *Derbyshire*, joined in 1935.

Canadian Pacific continued to dominate the great trans-Pacific route, between Vancouver and the Far East, with the addition of the 21,860grt *Empress of Australia* in 1920. Intended to be the *Tirpitz* for Hamburg America Line's transatlantic service to New York, she was never completed because of the war and then found her way, as part of reparations, into British hands. She joined the other well-reputed *Empress* liners, making the likes of ten-day passages between Vancouver and Shanghai with fares ranging from $350 in first class to $115 in so-called Asiatic steerage (the cost was even lower with Oriental food only). The *Empress of Australia*, which was one of the great rescue vessels of the horrific Tokyo earthquake of 1 September 1923, had joined the *Empress of Russia*, *Empress of Asia* and a fourth unit, a new-build, the 21,500grt *Empress of Canada*, which was completed in the spring of 1922.

Far from the likes of London, Liverpool and Southampton, the London-registered Union Steamship Company of New Zealand added the 17,500-ton *Aorangi* for their Pacific Ocean service between Sydney, Auckland and Vancouver. Then there was the *Razmak*, a large 10,600grt 'feeder ship' intended for P&O's shuttle service between Aden and Bombay and then used on the Marseilles–Bombay route. She was soon sold, however, going to the Union Steamship Co. of New Zealand, becoming the *Monowai* for the Sydney–San Francisco as well as the Wellington–Sydney services.

Indeed, British passenger ships sailed just about every sea lane.

four

GLORY DAYS:
NEW SHIPS OF THE 1930S

The tradition of naming a ship, especially a liner, has largely been the domain of women. But there were exceptions. The German kaiser, for example, named the giant *Imperator* (later Cunard's *Berengaria*) at her launching in 1911. Later, Canadian Pacific would ask the dashing, hugely popular Prince of Wales to do the honours for their largest liner of all, the *Empress of Britain*. Four years later, the prince's mother, Queen Mary, would name the biggest of all Cunarders.

The high pitch and bubbling ambition of the late 1920s led to enthusiastic planning by British ocean liner companies for the early 1930s. Both Cunard and White Star had planned super-liners by the time of the devastating Wall Street Crash in October 1929, and Canadian Pacific had also ordered big new liners for its Atlantic and Pacific services. Meanwhile, P&O ordered the first of its famed Strath liners – three-stackers that were reminders of the fabled Atlantic luxury liners. All except the projected White Star ship would materialise, but to the lean worrisome days of the worldwide Depression of the 1930s. There would be some devastating effects on the British liner business.

In what came to be the last hurrah for its trans-Pacific service, Canadian Pacific capped that trade with a large, luxurious, new three-stacker, the 26,000grt *Empress of Japan*, which was introduced in the summer of 1930. Immediately acclaimed as the finest liner to the Far East, she was also the fastest, making a record run from Victoria to Yokohama of seven days and twenty hours, and which was not surpassed until the 1960s. Later, in 1942 and after Imperial Japan entered the Second World War, the 1,173-passenger *Empress of Japan* was hurriedly renamed *Empress of Scotland*.

Canadian Pacific had, however, a far bigger, grander, even more notable liner on the way: the 42,300grt *Empress of Britain*, which was launched from the John Brown yard on the Clyde in June 1930 by the Prince of Wales (later Edward VIII and then the Duke of Windsor). The 758ft-long ship, delivered in May 1931, was the largest liner ever for the Canadian trade, sailing between Southampton and Quebec City. In winter, she was turned into the smartest of cruise ships, making annual four-month trips around the world with a reduced capacity and at a more leisurely speed. She was one of the ultimate ocean liners of the 1930s, capped by a trio of oversized gas-tank-like funnels. Unfortunately, she was not a huge success, either as an Atlantic liner or roving cruise ship.

But a far bigger ship was already well in the works by the time the *Empress of Britain* was commissioned. Between 1926 and 1928, Cunard Line planners diligently examined every aspect of contemporary marine engineering, design and decoration. Above all else, the intended new flagship of Cunard – together with a distantly projected sistership or running-mate – had to have the supreme competitive edge of offering the first ever twin-liner Atlantic express service. One ship would depart from Southampton as the other departed from New York and then pass one another somewhere in the mid-Atlantic. Even the ever-skilful Germans, with their new high-speed *Bremen* and *Europa*, commissioned in 1929–30, could not offer this prized commodity. Although they could cross between New York and the Channel ports in six days, the extension to and from Bremerhaven eliminated the chances of a twin-ship weekly service. A third ship, the somewhat smaller *Columbus* and actually something of a mismatch to the giant sisters, had to be worked into the schedules. Consequently, in this sense, the German team was hardly an improvement over the existing North Atlantic express threesomes, namely Cunard's *Aquitania*, *Berengaria* and *Mauretania* or White Star's grouping of the *Majestic*, *Olympic* and *Homeric*.

The overall design of the new Cunard express liner also had to meet any number of additional, quite specific requirements: prompt port turnarounds, continuous sailings for up to eleven months of each year (without major refits and repairs), substantial reserve power, strongly built to meet the rigours of the North Atlantic and a consistent operating speed of between 27½ and almost 29 knots (and faster, in fact, than any Blue Riband holder). Such a new ship would consume upwards of 11,000 tons of fuel per crossing compared to, say, the 3,800 tons for the *Mauretania* and the 5,000 tons for the *Berengaria*. Studies were also made for the choice of propulsion machinery (alone, fourteen different systems were considered including a latter-day use of coal) and while steam-turbine drive was the most likely (and eventually selected), even the then innovative and trendy turbo-electric type was given a rather serious look over. The French liked this method, in fact, and used it for their intended giant liner, the super-ship that was commissioned as the *Normandie* in 1935.

For the new Cunarder, there were tests and more tests, experiments, note-taking missions aboard other Cunarders as well as foreign-flag liners, small mountains of paperwork and reports, statistical studies and special examinations of such important liners as the *Aquitania*, the *Ile de France* and the new *Bremen*. There was even a large test sewage system, using glass tubes and coloured liquids, that was erected on the roof

Decorative splendour: the first-class gallery aboard the record-breaking *Empress of Japan* of 1930. *(Canadian Pacific)*

During a world cruise, the splendid-looking *Empress of Britain* passes under the Golden Gate Bridge at San Francisco. *(Canadian Pacific)*

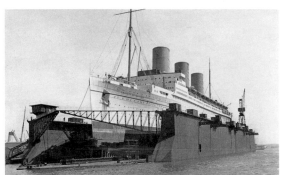

With her three oversized funnels, the 758ft-long *Empress of Britain* makes a very impressive sight while in the floating dock at Southampton. This view dates from 1932. *(Albert Wilhelmi Collection)*

The superb Cathay Lounge aboard the *Empress of Britain*. *(Albert Wilhelmi Collection)*

Finishing touches: the last section of the third funnel of the mighty *Empress of Britain* goes in place at the John Brown shipyard at Clydebank in 1931. *(Canadian Pacific)*

Cosy and inviting: the Knickerbocker Bar aboard the *Empress of Britain*. *(Richard Faber Collection)*

of the Cunard building in Liverpool. Each and every aspect of the new liner had to be considered and analysed: crew-members, engine spaces, kitchen designs, bedrooms, public rooms, storage, cargo handling, baggage, offices, hospital spaces and lesser details such as closet space for several vacuum cleaners. Expected to be near 80,000 tons, the new ship was unlike anything then in existence. Her needs and demands were extremely special. Every department at Cunard worked in close co-operation, often well into the night and behind lighted windows of the Liverpool headquarters. Saturdays and Sundays meant little; phone calls at two and three in the morning became normal.

The building order for this new ship was rather sensibly given to John Brown & Company Ltd, the famed Clydebank builders. The order was confirmed in May 1930. After all, John Brown had built the likes of the *Lusitania* in 1907 and then the *Aquitania* in 1914, the latter of which most strongly influenced the new giant's design and style. As work began on the big Cunarder, John Brown was busily finishing the 42,000-ton *Empress of Britain*, that startling new flagship of Canadian Pacific.

But a year or so later, in December 1931, the tide turned dramatically. Cunard was forced to halt construction of the new ship. Suddenly great gloom filled the company's boardrooms and offices. Due to the hideous Depression, the Cunard Company was about to realise a severe trading loss of 2.5 million for 1931. Overall, British passenger lines dropped from 9.1 million in 1928 to 3.9 million in 1931. Atlantic travel in first class alone fell at a startling rate – from 175,000 passengers in 1926 to 116,000 by 1931. Cunard was rightfully very worried. The most pressing problem was, of course, the large and costly new-build resting up on the Clydeside slipways. Questions arose: Should the project be stopped altogether? Or should it be sold off? And then if so, to whom? At the very worst, there were even rumours that the incomplete hull might be scrapped. Cunard had already spent £1.5 million on her. Monies were wasting every day and trading prospects for 1932 were worse still.

Once construction was officially halted, over 3,200 shipyard workers were sacked and at an untimely two weeks before Christmas. Another 10,000 workers from subsidiary companies were also affected. Only a bare staff of just over 400 remained at John Brown, but these were mostly draftsmen, senior crafts people and deputies. On the slipway, the huge steel frame of the liner sat like a naked barren skeleton: silent, rusting and nesting for birds.

Left, from top
Her Majesty Queen Mary, accompanied by His Majesty King George V, naming the *Queen Mary* at Clydebank on 26 September 1934. *(Albert Wilhelmi Collection)*

The 1,018ft-long *Queen Mary*, having just been launched, is carefully manoeuvred to the fitting-out basin at John Brown's yard. The Anchor liner *Tuscania* can be seen in the upper centre, serving as a spectator ship. *(Cronican-Arroyo Collection)*

Inbound at Southampton and heading for the King George V Graving Dock, the brand new *Queen Mary* passes the *Majestic* (left) and the *Windsor Castle* (right). *(Albert Wilhelmi Collection)*

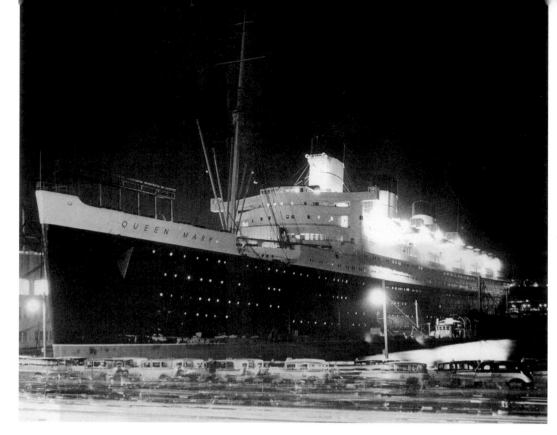

During her maiden call to New York in June 1936, the 81,200grt *Queen Mary* is aglow in lights. *(Cunard Line)*

High 1930s style: the sumptuous first-class gallery on board the *Queen Mary*. *(Albert Wilhelmi Collection)*

Good fortune later prevailed, however. The British Government offered assistance in the spring of 1934, but with some provisions and stipulations. In return for guaranteed loans to complete the new liner, Cunard would have to merge with its formal rival, the financially ailing White Star Line. To this Cunard readily agreed, and so inherited that company's ten passenger ships (joining Cunard's fifteen liners). Cunard-White Star Limited was promptly created. In return, Cunard received a three-part loan: £3 million to complete the new liner resting up on the Clyde, £5 million for a future running-mate and £1.5 million for much-needed emergency working capital. Quickly, on 3 April 1934, and after twenty-eight months of being idle, construction on the new ship, yard number 534, resumed. One of the first tasks was to remove some 130 tons of rust on the steel frames of the 1,018ft-long hull.

In the months ahead, one of the more pressing questions was to find a name for the new ship. The likes of *Britannia*, *Galicia*, *Hamptonia*, *Clydania* and then *Princess Elizabeth*, *Princess Margaret Rose* and even *Marina* (for Princess Marina) were said to be considered. But the most persistent tale is that Cunard directors preferred *Victoria*. In the end, and in respect to those stoic icons of a quickly vanishing age, King George V and Queen Mary, the name *Queen Mary* was chosen. The old Queen, often seen sitting and standing bolt upright and wearing long Victorian-era dresses, choker pearls and toque hats, was said to be honoured and delighted with the new ship bearing her name.

Deep in those Depression years, the building of the ship had taken on unintended symbolism. As Britain's brilliant 'ship of state', she was a project of fortitude and determination, of an otherwise struggling weary nation overcoming the havoc and despair of those lean years. She was also the centrepiece of enormous pride, superb workmanship, advanced design, great power and the combined efforts of so many. The liner was also a link between levels of British society – from the royal family and Government officials to artisans and designers to grimy-faced riveters and pipe fitters.

The King and the Queen, together with the dashing Prince of Wales, entrained from their Highland retreat at Balmoral for Clydebank on 26 September 1934. It was the day of the formal launching. It was the very first time that a reigning British Queen was to name a merchant ship. In due course, both her daughter-in-law (Queen Elizabeth) and her granddaughter (Queen Elizabeth II) would do the same. From behind a glass shield on the launch platform, at just after three in the afternoon, Queen Mary – looking out onto a blanket of some 200,000 umbrellas huddled under Scottish rain – released a bottle of Australian wine into the great bow of the liner. Within her twenty-eight words, her first public speech as Queen consort, she announced the ship's name to the public for the first time. Great, enthusiastic cheers went up!

Thousands more spectators watched the launch from the opposite shore of the Clyde and still others were aboard the specially moored liner *Tuscania* of the Anchor Line, which had been chartered to serve as a floating grandstand. Within fifty-five seconds, the 30,000-ton shell of the *Queen Mary* was waterborne. Life for the *Mary*, as she would be affectionately known, had begun. So delighted, George V called her 'the stateliest ship in being'.

It took another eighteen months to fit out the liner and prepare her for commissioning in the spring of 1936. In the end, the *Mary* was ready for appraisal. Despite touches of modern art placed mostly in the public lounges, she was a conservative liner, one very much in the tradition of a fine but well-established hotel. She was said to be a warm and comfortable ship, with less of the massive grander tones of, say, France's *Normandie*, her nearest rival. The Cunarder lacked the high glitter, the almost pretentious extravagance of the French flagship. Both inside and out, the *Mary* followed very much in the spirit and wake of earlier Cunarders, namely the *Aquitania*, which dated from 1914. On board the new liner, there were soft sofas and upholstered armchairs, pylon lamps and fireplaces, glossy veneers, chromium and glass lighting fixtures, carpets of florals and swirls, brass handrails and wood-framed clocks, great murals and velvet drapes, and a mounted marble medallion depicting the Queen. Above all else, the *Mary* was unmistakably a British ship, assuredly a Cunarder. She was the perfect evolutionary ship and far less revolutionary than even Cunard publicists liked to suggest.

Not all Britons reached for a pen to write of her praises, however. She was quite contemporary, even modern to many. To some, her passenger spaces too often resembled a Leicester Square cinema. To others she was said to be too 'teddy bear'. One critic went so far as to label her first-class public rooms as being 'Woolworth five-and-dime'. One subsequently complained that some of her lounges had all the severity of the Palace of Culture in Warsaw.

No fewer than eighteen special excursion trains carried thousands down to the Southampton Docks on 26 May 1936. Ships, tugs and other craft crammed the Solent and formed an enormous send-off flotilla for the sparkling new *Queen Mary*. The strains of *Rule Britannia* rang out. Scores of journalists and photographers were on hand, later sending their prized results by train as well as car to their anxious Fleet Street editors. One enterprising London photographer, who I met forty years later during a Mediterranean cruise on board the *Canberra*, claimed to have delivered the very first photographs of the departing *Queen Mary*. Cleverly, his undeveloped rolls of film were sent from the Southampton countryside by carrier pigeon.

Some 1,849 passengers were aboard for the maiden run to New York. Their fares ranged from fifty in cabin class (renamed from first class in the late 1930s), twenty-eight in tourist class (the former cabin class) and eighteen in third class (post-war tourist class). When she reached New York, to a wildly enthusiastic welcome, *The New York Times* reported, 'A gentle blizzard of torn paper appeared in the great canyons between the buildings, bursting on the hot summer air as suddenly and as decoratively as a flight of pigeons.'

Two months later, in August, the *Queen Mary* captured the Blue Riband with a run of just three minutes under four days. She outpaced the *Normandie* with an average speed 30.68 knots. Cunard was, however, quite casual about the achievement of their new liner. They even declined a special welcome at Southampton (but a grand reception assembled just the same). A company spokesman was rather offhand by saying: 'It's all

in a day's work for us.' Content with his efforts, a proud chief engineer remarked, 'I think we should all be surprised if we really opened her out.' From Malta, during a yachting cruise, Edward VIII wired: 'Sincere congratulations on the *Queen Mary*'s fine record.'

Immensely popular and even quite profitable from the start, the *Queen Mary* was not without her problems. She suffered a common ill to very big liners: very noticeable and strong vibrations. This required considerable alteration and change to both her structuring and her propellers. The ship's huge steel framework had to be reinforced during her first winter overhaul in January 1937. Extra steel beams had to be inserted, others strengthened and the bilge keels widened. Entire lounges and cabins had to be stripped to bare steel in the process. Much of the fine, glossy oak panels had to be removed as well. They were systematically numbered, stored ashore and then reinserted.

The propellers were also found to be faulty. Since eight propellers had been created for the quadruple-screw liner (four for use and four for reserve), the spare set was temporarily installed while the original quartet were taken ashore and altered. They were eventually discarded, however. A new set of fresh design was built and, after considerable testing, showed a marked improvement in the performance of the *Queen Mary*.

The Cunarder was also a rather notorious, sometimes worrisome roller, especially in those severe autumn and winter Atlantic gales. One frequent joke was, 'the *Queen Mary* could roll the milk out of a cup of tea!' One crew-member later recounted: 'I was thrown out of my bunk on board the *Mary* and thought the ship was never coming back [righting herself]. I recall thinking "this was the end. She can never come back from that angle."' On another early voyage many passengers became quite hysterical as the liner rolled continuously. Heavy and hard rolling for the *Queen Mary* was a problem for most of her sea-going career.

The *Mary* lost the Blue Riband in March 1937 to the *Normandie*, which had an average speed of 30.9 knots. The French liner later advanced to a record of 31.2 knots. The Cunarder finally and firmly retook the title, however, in August 1938. Then her average speed was 31.6 knots, with a record crossing of three days, twenty hours and forty-two minutes. The *Mary* held the honour of being the world's fastest liner for fourteen years, until July 1952, when it was taken by the final Blue Riband holder, the very advanced *United States*.

The White Star Line never quite recovered from the loss of the *Titanic* in 1912. By the 1920s, the company grew increasingly fragile. They did, however, plan for a super-liner, the 60,000grt *Oceanic*, at the very end of that decade. She was to have been paired with another giant liner, the 81,000-tonner that would become Cunard's *Queen Mary*. But soon after the shattering Wall Street Crash in October 1929, White Star fell on even harder financial times. Almost immediately, the *Oceanic* project, which was nothing more than keel plates at the Harland & Wolff yard at Belfast, was cancelled. Instead, two more moderate ships were given the green light, the 27,000-ton *Britannic* and her near-sister the *Georgic*. A squat-stacked motor-liner, the 712ft-long *Britannic* was commissioned in the spring of 1930. But the brightness and high spirits of her introduction were dimmed somewhat by the dark, quickly gathering clouds of the worldwide Depression. Like so many other passenger ships, the *Britannic* would have to struggle to fill all her passenger berths in the ensuing years.

The smart-looking *Britannic* arriving at the Princes Landing Stage at Liverpool. (*Albert Wilhelmi Collection*)

Great shipboard comfort: The first-class long gallery aboard the *Britannic*. (*Richard Faber Collection*)

While undergoing repairs from a prior fire at Hamilton, the 19,000grt *Bermuda* burns for a second time while undergoing repairs at Belfast. (*Cronican-Arroyo Collection*)

A splendid three-stacker, the *Queen of Bermuda* departs from Hamilton for New York. (*Albert Wilhelmi Collection*)

In sleek moderne, the *Britannic* was a long low ship with two very low funnels (only the second one actually worked; the forward one housed a wireless and radio room) and had a raked bow and classic cruiser stern. Danish-built Burmeister & Wain diesels were connected to twin propellers. Passenger berths totalled 1,553 in three classes and then there was considerable cargo space, carried in less than seven holds. Transatlantic crossings (between Liverpool and later London to New York) were paired with periodic Caribbean as well as long Mediterranean cruises.

Away from the 'big ships' of the North Atlantic run, the Furness-Bermuda Line developed a keen interest and great success in the holiday trade between New York and Bermuda, a voyage of a mere 600 miles in each direction. In the wake of second-hand tonnage, they soon looked, by 1927, to building larger, more luxurious tonnage – namely the 19,000grt, 691-passenger *Bermuda*. A handsome, popular ship, she was also most unfortunate. She burned out at Bermuda when only three years old, then burned again and sank during her repairs at Belfast, and even went aground in the end when her scorched remains were being towed off to the scrappers at Rosyth in Scotland. Her replacement, the 22,500grt *Monarch of Bermuda*, was an even finer ship, 'like a trans-Atlantic liner, especially with her three funnels and beautiful public rooms', recalled the late Everett Viez, a liner enthusiast. She spawned a near-sister, the *Queen of Bermuda*, in 1933 and together they were two of the most popular and profitable British liners of the 1930s.

In 1931, the Pacific Steam Navigation Co. Ltd added the superb *Reina Del Pacifico*, a 17,700grt motor-liner with squat stacks, a white hull and fine quarters for 888 passengers in three classes. She traded on the Liverpool–west coast of South America run and was a long-time favourite, offering the likes of forced-air ventilation, a complete hair salon and even an American bar.

P&O also used an all-white look for its newest and largest liners to date, the 22,500-ton sisters *Strathnaver* and *Strathaird*. Used on the Australian run, they too used the three-funnel system to remind the public of larger, usually Atlantic liners. Two of the funnels were dummies actually, but used to good effect. They were classic-looking liners and led to three more quite similar ships, the *Strathmore*, the *Strathallan* and *Stratheden*, beginning in 1935. The late Laurence Dunn once noted:

> Vickers, while a fine shipbuilder, designed ships, including passenger liners, more from a technical point of view rather than aesthetic. There was no attempt at streamlining or even exterior elegance. There was great continuity with P&O's Strath liners [1931–32], Orient Line's *Orion* [1935] and, in post-war, with the likes of the *Orcades*, *Oronsay*, *Orsova* and *Oriana*. Clearly, the *Himalaya* [1949] was a continuation of the *Stratheden* [1937].

P&O also reinforced its London–Far East passenger service, primarily to colonial Singapore and Hong Kong, with new sisterships, the *Corfu* and *Carthage* of 1931, and then with a larger finer version, the *Canton* of 1939.

The rival Orient Line was more innovative. When adding the 23,300-ton *Orion* and her near-sister, the *Orcades*, in 1935, they brought the sleek look of Art Deco to the UK–Australia trade. Her public rooms had a clean, sleek look and which was accentuated by highly polished lino floors. She was a great reminder of the famed Atlantic liners of

The two-deck-high dining room aboard the *Queen of Bermuda*. *(Frank O. Braynard Collection)*

The first-class smoking room aboard the *Strathnaver*. *(Richard Faber Collection)*

The all-white *Reina Del Pacifico* passing through the Panama Canal. *(Albert Wilhelmi Collection)*

Comfort to Australia: the first-class verandah cafe, also aboard the *Strathnaver*. *(Richard Faber Collection)*

Grand setting: the gentlemen's club room aboard the *Reina Del Pacifico*. *(Richard Faber Collection)*

Every amenity: the well-fitted children's playroom in first class aboard the *Stratheden*. *(Richard Faber Collection)*

P&O's *Strathaird* and her sister *Strathnaver* were given three funnels (the first and third were dummy stacks) so as to resemble larger liners. *(Richard Faber Collection)*

that same period. 'The *Orion* was unique since she was named [on 7 December 1934] by the Duke of Gloucester, who was in Brisbane at the time,' noted Lindsay Johnstone:

The event was relayed by radio to the Vickers shipyard in England. When she was first commissioned, she was such an innovative ship, so Art Deco for the Aussie run. She had long white columns in the lounge and tubular chairs. To us in Sydney, she was like one of the famous Atlantic super liners. She also started the use of lighter, corn-coloured hull colouring for future Orient Line ships. This was innovative. I saw the Orion in her later years, but she had faded by then. She was showing her age.

The 23,400grt *Strathmore*, completed in 1935, at the Tilbury landing stage, London. The *Viceroy of India*, *Ranpura* and *Laurentic* are moored in the upper background. (P&O)

For military connections throughout the empire, but often out to the Far East and, of course, just in case of war, a quartet of four 11,000-ton, purposeful peacetime troopships were created between 1936 and 1939. Chartered to the Ministry of Transport in London and used on occasion for budget cruises as well, British India Line operated two, the *Dilwara* and *Dunera*. P&O managed the *Ettrick* while Bibby Line took over the last of the four, the 517ft-long *Devonshire*.

Union-Castle decided to accelerate as well as enhance its Southampton–Cape express service and so added the 25,500grt sisters *Stirling Castle* and *Athlone Castle* in 1935–36, which were followed by the slightly larger *Capetown Castle* in 1938. Noted for their long low superstructures, flattish funnels and their eye-catching lavender-coloured hulls, they were appraised as three of the most handsome liners in the otherwise huge British fleet.

In the autumn of 1936, Ellerman Lines added its finest liner to date, the 219-passenger, all-first-class *City of Benares*. An 11,000-tonner with twin funnels and so looking much like a mini-liner, she was used on the London–Bombay route.

Away from its North Atlantic service, the Anchor Line remained keenly interested in the colonial service to India and Pakistan, and so added three new motor-liners, *Circassia* and *Cilicia*, in 1937–38. A third duplicate ship, the *Caledonia*, joined a decade later, after the Second World War, in 1948.

It wasn't all carefree days and brand new passenger ships during the Depression-ridden 1930s, of course. Beginning in 1930, and to avoid the harsh possibilities of either of lay-up or, worse still, premature retirement and scrapping, big ships such as Cunard's *Aquitania* were sent on more and more revenue-earning cruises. These included, from

New York, $10 overnight trips 'to nowhere'. They sailed out to sea and back just for the night. Passing the legal three-mile limit and thereby avoiding the harsh restrictions of American Prohibition, the ship's bars were open legally to otherwise thirsty Americans. Thus, these short voyages were also dubbed 'booze cruises'.

'Cunard was a great, well known shipping line back in the '30s and the service on board, even in those lean Depression years, was top-class,' remembered Victor Newman, who was a passenger on a four-and-a-half-day cruise up to Halifax and back to New York:

We sailed at midnight, with great festivity and a big band playing on deck, on a Friday. The cruise was advertised as a 'long weekend away.' It was $45 per person in the cheapest cabin. What a thrill to sail on the famous *Aquitania*. She was such a wonderful ship and a great 'sea boat' as well!

British cruising also became very popular in the otherwise hard-pressed 1930s. Many lines and their ships were sent off on leisure voyages, some offering rates as low as one per day for 'escapist' jaunts to the Canaries, Spain and Portugal, into the Mediterranean, to the Norwegian fjords and around the northern cities. Leslie Shaw, a Londoner, sailed in the mid-1930s on two Canadian Pacific passenger ships, the *Montcalm* and *Montclare* – 16,400-tonners that were normally on the North Atlantic run between Liverpool, Quebec City and Montreal:

These very ordinary ships offered standard tourist class cruises. There were no added frills, no great glamour and the ships themselves were quite basic. They offered 14-night cruises from Southampton to Gibraltar, Algiers, Barcelona and Ceuta. They were appealing because it was well before 'odd places' as ports of call came into fashion. The fares began at £13 for a lower-deck quad and as much as £16 for an upper-deck single.

There were shorter cruise-like voyages as well. 'In 1937, I took the train from London to the south of France for a holiday,' recalled Leslie Shaw. 'But I came home from Marseilles to London on the *Narkunda* of P&O, a ship returning from a long voyage out to India.'

But sometimes cruises had added excitement. In August 1935, Leslie Shaw made a two-week cruise to the Mediterranean aboard Cunard-White Star's *Doric*. 'The voyage started off quite happily, but the return was quite unintended,' he recalled during an interview some forty years later, aboard the P&O cruise ship *Sea Princes*:

About 40 miles off Oporto in Portugal, we collided [in fog] with a French steamer, the *Formigny*. I had gone to bed just after the cinema presentation that night, but was awakened at three in the morning. Women and some blind ex-soldiers were the first to be placed in the lifeboats of the badly damaged, listing *Doric*. We were in the thickest fog, on a dead flat sea and already listing seven or eight degrees. We were not in immediate danger, so it seemed, and boarding the boats was slow and quite orderly. I carried my own case into the lifeboat at 8 the following morning. There was 800 of us, all being sent to one of the nearby passenger ships that offered assistance and rescue.

The launch at Vickers of Barrow-in-Furness of the *Stratheden* on 10 June 1937. *(P&O)*

The single-funnel *Orion* anchored at Balholm, Norway, during a summertime cruise from London to the spectacular Fjords. *(Albert Wilhelmi Collection)*

Built for the London–Far East service in 1939, the *Canton* was a very handsome ship; a refinement in ways of the earlier *Strath* liners and the sisters *Corfu* and *Carthage* of 1931. *(P&O)*

High Art Deco on the high seas and to Australia: the first-class main lounge aboard the *Orion* of 1935. *(P&O)*

The new 725ft-long, 20-knot *Stirling Castle* seen departing from Southampton for Cape Town in a view dated 30 May 1936. *(Cronican-Arroyo Collection)*

With only one of her four funnels remaining, the *Mauretania* is being dismantled in this view from the top of the hammerhead crane at Rosyth. *(Richard Faber Collection)*

Left, from top
End of the line: the veteran *Mauretania* passes under the Firth of Forth Bridge in 1935, bound for the scrappers at nearby Rosyth. *(Cronican-Arroyo Collection)*

HMS *Caledonia*, the former *Majestic* and once the largest ship afloat, is towed into Rosyth for use as an Admiralty cadet training ship. Note the Firth of Forth Bridge on the far left. The ship's funnels and masts have been especially cut down in height. *(Albert Wilhelmi Collection)*

Brand new in the winter of 1939, the smart-looking *Dominion Monarch* passes the famed *Cutty Sark* and, at the far left, the training ship *Worcester* in the Thames. *(Albert Wilhelmi Collection)*

Festive occasion: the *Mauretania* departing from Liverpool on her maiden voyage in June 1939. *(G.D. Watt Collection)*

Four-hundred went to Orient Line's brand new *Orion*. Along with the other 400, I went to P&O's *Viceroy of India*, which days later delivered me to the Tilbury Docks at London. I especially recall that first breakfast. She was my first P&O of many ships.

Escapist cruising on ships included the rather luxurious, certainly clubby, high-end likes of Blue Star Line's 15,500grt, 354-berth *Arandora Star* and the 15,600grt, 450-bed *Atlantis* of Royal Mail Lines. They were considered Britain's finest and most popular cruise ships of the 1930s, sailing in summers to Norway and the northern cities, and otherwise to the Mediterranean, the Atlantic Isles, West Africa and, on shorter itineraries, down to Spain and Portugal. Their passenger lists included business executives and aristocrats, even minor royalty on occasion.

The likes of the stately *Aquitania* endured, aged and creaking. She made more cruises, including longer more luxurious trips around the Mediterranean and to Rio de Janeiro for the annual carnival, along with Atlantic crossings. The *Aquitania* was to be retired in 1940, as the new *Queen Elizabeth* came into service. But the outbreak of the Second World War, on 1 September 1939, changed all that. The twenty-five-year-old four-stacker was kept around, serving as a grey-painted troopship for the second time.

By the late 1930s, those great floating palaces from pre-First World War days had all but disappeared. The likes of the *Homeric*, *Olympic*, *Mauretania* and *Berengaria* went quietly, if sentimentally, to the breakers. The case of the *Majestic* was more prolonged. She was yanked from Cunard-White Star service in the winter of 1936, losing money as well as passengers and in anticipation of the arrival in May of the new *Queen Mary*, and then sold for $400,000 for British ship-breakers. There was some rethinking, however, and she was soon resold to the British Admiralty for use as a cadets' training ship for 1,500 boys and 500 officer apprentices. She was renamed HMS *Caledonia* and sent to moorings at Rosyth in Scotland. She remained there until the outbreak of war in September 1939, when her trainees were reassigned to shore-side quarters. For a time she was moored in the Firth of Forth with her fate uncertain; unlikely to return to sea-going service, she had a sad ending instead. She caught fire on 29 September 1939, burned out and then partially sank. Salvage began months later, in March 1940, and then the hulk was towed to nearby Inverkeithing for slow demolition, which was not completed for more than three years.

Several important passenger ships emerged almost on the eve of war. Cunard wanted a relief ship, one capable of making seven-night passages between Southampton and New York, for its intended pairing of the super-liners *Queen Mary* and *Queen Elizabeth*. This came in the form of the 35,700grt *Mauretania*, built by Cammell Laird of Birkenhead and therefore ranking as the largest liner yet built in England. She was an immediate success and ranks as a favourite Cunarder. A 772ft-long liner, she was also the largest to visit the Port of London. The late P.J. Branch, an engineer with the Port of London Authority, recalled the visit of the *Mauretania* in the summer of 1939 to the London Docks. 'She was the largest ship of any kind, liner or otherwise, to enter the locks at London. It was a major event. She was so big that she flooded the Thames River banks with her wash, however.'

Shaw Savill added its largest and finest liner to date in the winter of 1939, in the form of the 27,100grt *Dominion Monarch*. Carrying just 517 passengers in all first-class quarters, she was used on the long-haul run between London and Southampton to Fremantle, Melbourne and Sydney, and then over to Auckland and Wellington, and all by way of the South African Cape, via Cape Town and Durban. She was immediately appraised by many as the finest ship on the Aussie run. Australian ship enthusiast Clifford Hocking remembered the *Dominion Monarch*: 'She was a very special ship that had architectural features. She had columned lounges, for example, that were almost Corinthian. On the inside, she looked like London clubs. She was really quite grand.' Another Australian enthusiast Lindsay Johnstone added: 'She had the most beautiful, two-deck high dining room. She was also very popular in Australia being the fastest liner of her time on the run to and from the UK.'

Royal Mail Lines was also crowning its fleet and its run to the east coast of America with the 25,600grt, Belfast-built *Andes*. Launched in March 1939, her maiden voyage was set for 26 September which, as events progressed, was over three weeks after the start of the Second World War. The trip was cancelled and, beginning that December, the 669ft-long liner completed instead as a grey-coloured troopship. Her maiden trip to Latin America would be delayed by almost nine years, until January 1948.

five

CALL TO DUTY: SERVICE IN THE SECOND WORLD WAR

On 1 September 1939, the glittering lights of Europe suddenly went out as the Nazis dramatically and ferociously slammed into Poland. Britain was soon at war. Preparations were now paramount. Among others, almost all British passenger ships were called to duty, requisitioned by the Government and called up for more pressing military duties, usually trooping. The senses of urgency and emergency were immediate. On 3 September the 13,400-ton *Athenia* of Glasgow's Donaldson Line was torpedoed and sunk by a German U-boat off the Hebrides. There were 112 casualties among the passengers and crew. The British Government was stunned, the public shocked. British shipping, the wonderful, pleasure-filled liners included, were again at war.

British passenger ships were immediately pressed into varied services, mostly becoming grey-painted troopships but also serving as armed merchant cruisers, small aircraft carriers, hospitals, floating repair shops and, later, even as targets for Royal Navy practice sessions. The Government, using the fine skills of British shipowners, managed many foreign-flag ships during the war. These included the French *Ile de France* and *Pasteur*, Holland's *Nieuw Amsterdam*, Norway's *Bergensfjord* and Greece's *Nea Hellas*. Overall, British passenger ships and those operated by the British gave valiant, heroic service during the war. The *Queen Mary* and *Queen Elizabeth* were perhaps the most notable, ferrying 2 million mostly American, British and Canadian military personnel across the North Atlantic between January 1942 and, after the peace, well into 1946. Famously, Prime Minister Winston Churchill said the Cunard Queens helped to end the war in Europe by at least a year.

However, between September 1939 and the summer of 1945, over 800,000 tons of British shipping was lost. Some 30,000 merchant seamen lost their lives. The most horrific loss was perhaps that of Cunard's *Lanastria*, then serving as a troopship and which was attacked by Nazi bombers during the evacuation of western France in June 1940. She took four strategic hits, including a bomb down her funnel, and quickly sank with over 5,000 casualties. In October that year, the 42,300grt *Empress of Britain* was sunk by Nazi bombers and later torpedoed as well while homeward bound off the Irish coast. She ranked as the largest Allied merchant ship to be sunk during the Second World War. Other noted losses included the likes of P&O's *Viceroy of India* and *Strathallan*, Orient Line's *Orcades* and the *Windsor Castle* of Union-Castle. Others, such as White Star's *Georgic* and Royal Mail's *Asturias*, were thought to be lost but then survived and endured extensive repairs and eventual rehabilitation.

The great effort at sea continued, of course. Cunard crewman Richard Gibson first went to sea in June 1943. His first assignment was the grey-painted *Franconia*. 'At the time, the *Franconia* was trooping to Sicily and my first trip was with 42 other converted liners, all them going out to Algiers in a huge convoy,' he remembered:

> I started as a deck boy and received £2.50 a month. There was 10 monthly allowance for 'danger money'. We had 3,000 troops on board. Her port engines had been damaged and so we had to make do with only one engine, making a scant 10–11 knots, but which was actually adequate for our convoy, which travelled at a very slow and cautious 8 knots. After delivering the troops and then continuing onward to Malta, we left the convoy and returned to the UK with only one escort ship. It was a rather dangerous voyage with U-boats lurking just about everywhere. The *Franconia* was then laid-up for repairs, for 4½ months, off Gareloch Head in Scotland. Once these were completed, we resumed trooping, but on the North Atlantic, between Gourock and Halifax & New York.

Douglass Campbell, who later travelled aboard many passenger ships, including many of the great liners, had his very first voyage in December 1943. It was a free trip, courtesy of the US government. As a young soldier, he was sent off on a twenty-one-day voyage from Newport News, Virginia to Bombay via Cape Town. He was aboard Canadian Pacific's converted *Empress of Scotland*. 'We zig-zagged all the way, the ship crammed with soldiers,' he recalled:

> I was assigned to the former children's playroom with bunks three high. While the ship was well provisioned, we had to conserve water use and endured tremendous heat, especially below decks, in southern waters. Life among the soldiers was very simple, but there was always a sense of some tension. Rumours would spring up of lurking enemy subs and, of course, a big liner serving as an Allied troopship was a prime target.

Leslie Shaw was sent to North Africa early in the war and remembered, 'I was sent out from Liverpool to Algiers on an especially long 19-day trip in a convoy in a converted Canadian Pacific liner, the *Duchess of York*. She rolled and pitched so often that she was

Great escape: the incomplete *Queen Elizabeth* flees from the Clyde to the safety of New York in February 1940. *(Richard Faber Collection)*

Safe arrival in New York: the grey-painted *Queen Elizabeth* arrives in New York for the first time in March 1940. The *Queen Mary* and the *Normandie* are to the left. *(Albert Wilhelmi Collection)*

soon dubbed "the Drunken Duchess". There were 5,000 on board, mostly British Army riflemen and soldiers.'

Miss Billie Ellis was a first lieutenant in the US Army during the peak years of the Second World War, in 1943. Recently, aboard the Cunard liner *Queen Victoria*, she recalled a voyage in another Cunarder: aboard the *Mauretania* in 1943. That 1939-built ship was then far from her luxurious self, being painted entirely in sombre grey for use as an Allied troopship. She shipped out in January 1943, but far from the 35,600grt ship's intended run on the Atlantic, between New York and Southampton, the 23-knot Cunard vessel was routed, in top wartime secrecy, from Southampton:

> I had been delivered to the *Mauretania* by a US Army tender. The *Mauretania* looked huge to me. Once aboard, she still retained some of her pre-war luxuries – the walnut panels that were just magnificent. She was actually stripped down except for the dining room, but there were hints of grandeur. We were a very crowded ship with 9,000 on board. Even the drained pool was used for sleeping quarters. The officers were given the staterooms while the troops used big, specially created dormitories. There were six to eight nurses aboard along with eighteen doctors. I was assigned to a two-berth room that was now sleeping six, but we still had use of the beautiful bathroom. I remember, however, that the soap would not lather because we only had saltwater.

> It was forty-eight days from San Francisco all the way to Bombay. We made several stops, including Wellington in New Zealand. But no one was allowed ashore. It was all top secret. We were not even told we were headed for India.

> I was one of the nurses that helped run the ship's hospital. The hospital was always very busy. There was a rather large hospital in one of the converted public rooms and where

there were actual beds instead of cots. There was also a small operating room. We had lots of medical problems. It was so busy that we did not feel the intense heat on board. After New Zealand, we stopped at Brisbane and then Perth in Australia. We were not in a convoy and did not have an escort, and so it was very frightening at times. At times, it was said that Japanese submarines were trailing us. But we were travelling so fast that the subs, so it was said, could not catch us. The ship vibrated very much. There was no radar back then and, of course, we were blacked out and radio silent. We arrived in Bombay in March.

Three small passenger ships took Billie Ellis to ports along the Persian Gulf to serve troops suffering mostly from malaria and severe dysentery. She was also transported on the passenger ship *Rohna*, which belonged to the British India Line. After three and a half years in the Gulf and in Russia, she herself later contracted malaria and dysentery. She was sent home from Europe by way of the North Atlantic:

> I was sent home on another troopship, the *Hermitage*, which departed from Marseilles. We had many of the American soldiers that had been in the German prison camps. There were often very sick and many were so ill that they died.

> We were to sail home to Boston, but were rerouted to New York … As we entered New York harbour, we stood on deck in full uniform and were moved to tears as we passed the Statue of Liberty. The decks were lined from end to end with troops. Coming home on the *Hermitage* was very, very emotional.

There were special occasions even during the war. In the winter of 1945, the troopship *Franconia* was selected as the possible host ship for a special, history-making conference. According to crewman Richard Gibson:

Wartime exploits: crowds gather along the quayside at Montevideo, Uruguay, in December 1940 to view the auxiliary cruiser *Carnarvon Castle*, a converted Union-Castle liner, arriving after a battle with a German raider. *(Cronican-Arroyo Collection)*

Crowds welcome the troopship *Otranto* at Fremantle in September 1945. *(Albert Wilhelmi Collection)*

Still in wartime dress: the *Empress of Scotland*, carrying troops, visits Valletta and Malta, in a view dated 16 February 1948. *(Michael Cassar Collection)*

We had been on leave at Liverpool when suddenly all hands were asked to return immediately. We found that the *Franconia* had been partially stripped and then rebuilt in places. The big lounges, for example, had been made soundproof, the suites had been restored and refurbished, and some peacetime, luxury pieces of furniture had been brought out of wartime storage. Also, the crew bar had been transformed into a massive radio and communications centre. We later discovered that the ship might be used for the entire Yalta Conference if no other suitable location was available at that Black Sea port. Churchill, Roosevelt and Stalin would be coming aboard.

Soon, the *Franconia* departed from Liverpool. 'In disguise, we carried some naval troops out to the Dardanelles and, since we were still painted overall in greys, we looked quite like any other ordinary troop carrier,' recalled Gibson:

Churchill flew down to Yalta, joined the ship for his accommodations and then we moved to Sevastopol, where only two buildings had been left standing. A banquet was held on board, but there was little formal use after that. Plans changed. Churchill, Stalin and Roosevelt used the ship as a group for only one day. After that, the *Franconia* resumed trooping, carrying British forces home from Bombay to Liverpool and then ferrying South African servicemen down to the Cape. She was not returned to Cunard until the summer of 1947 and then restored for return to peacetime service.

The *Empress of Russia*, with stern gun mountings, as seen in a view dating from 1941. *(Cronican-Arroyo Collection)*

six

BOOM TIMES: HEYDAY OF THE 1950S

In October 1947, a young Princess Elizabeth, accompanied by the Duke of Edinburgh, travelled to the John Brown shipyard in Clydebank, to name Britain's newest, largest and most luxurious post-war liner. She went down the ways as the *Caronia*, a 34,200-tonner that symbolised Britain's return and revival in the liner trades more than any other ship. Although Britain was all but bankrupt by the war's end, in the summer of 1945 the nation launched an almost immediate post-war boom in shipbuilding, ship repairs and restoration. Within three years, almost every British shipping company had new tonnage either in the works or being commissioned.

The 715ft-long *Caronia* could carry 932 passengers, divided between 581 in first class and 351 in cabin class, but with the novelty of every cabin having a private bathroom. A palatial ship, done in a grand but most comfortable clubby style, she was unique for several reasons: the largest liner to date with a single mast; the largest with a single funnel; and being painted entirely in shades of green. She was soon dubbed the 'Green Goddess'. But she was also unique in being largely intended for long, luxurious cruises, four to fourteen weeks of sailing the world and with her capacity purposely reduced to a more intimate 600. She was soon appraised as the finest cruise ship afloat and, by many, as the very finest Cunarder. Mary Plunkett, a passenger on her world cruises, recalled, 'She was like a great country house. Everything was perfect, polished, absolutely impeccable! Many of us thought she was the finest, best-run ship in the world.'

In a break from its large liner preferences, Cunard also added two combination passenger-cargo ships, the 13,300-grt *Media* and *Parthia*, for its Liverpool–New York service. Notably, when the 530ft-long *Media* was commissioned in August 1947, she was the very first brand new passenger ship on the Atlantic run following the war.

Unquestionably the most popular, successful and publicised super-liners afloat following the Second World War were the Cunard Queens, the immortal *Queen Mary* and *Queen Elizabeth*. They were, in fact, always thought of as a pair, simply as 'the Queens'. Many thought they were identical sisters. Instead, they were actually quite different ships. The *Mary* was a three-stacker, older, even old-fashioned, a speed champion and beloved by passengers and crew alike. The *Elizabeth* was a twin-stacker, more contemporary, raked, perhaps slightly less grand and never quite as warmly loved as her running-mate. A charming story from aboard the *Queen Mary* concerns a rich Texan seated in the Verandah Grill restaurant. So delighted with the food, the service

and the overall style of the ship, he asked if he might buy the *Queen*. A rather surprised maître d' supposedly responded, 'I'm terribly sorry, sir, but you see she's part of a set.'

London-based P.J. Branch added: 'The *Queen Mary* and *Queen Elizabeth* were never, ever ordinary ships. British people were very proud of them. They added prestige to the Empire. And they were held in affection, often great affection, not only by the British people, but the British maritime trades as well.'

The two giant Cunarders were favoured by many Atlantic travellers, New Yorker Douglass Campbell among them. He made numerous crossings on both the *Queen Mary* and *Queen Elizabeth*, and recalled:

> First class was very luxurious on the Queens. It was always black tie for dinner. Every piece of your clothing was laid down beforehand and your shoes always freshly polished. There was a steward as well as a stewardess to every stateroom. The tubs had four knobs, saltwater as well as fresh. Young boys wearing pillbox hats delivered lots of messages since the inter-cabin phone system was limited. There was no ship-to-shore, but wireless for long-distance messages. The food was extremely good, with lots of roasts and birds. It was all very English and always beautifully served. The menus were quite extensive and, of course, you paid extra for dinner in the Verandah Grill.

In particular, the *Queen Mary* still suffered from an infirmity: great rolling when at sea. Douglass Campbell was aboard for an off-season crossing in December 1947 and recalled: 'There were no stabilisers back then and the ship, even the giant *Queen Mary*, rolled tremendously. Cunard waiters used to soak the tablecloths just to keep the dishes from sliding off the tables.'

The old White Star Line house-flag and funnel colours also reappeared on the Atlantic after the war. The *Britannic* returned but to Cunard-White Star's luxury passenger service in 1948, after spending six years as a troopship during the Second World War. Refurbished, her peacetime quarters were restyled for 429 in first class and 569 in tourist class. She spent about ten months of the year on crossings between Liverpool and New York, with a stop at Cobh in each direction, and an annual long Mediterranean–Black Sea cruise from New York became a highlight. Minimum fares for these sixty-six-day voyages, which departed in January, were priced from $1,000 in the 1950s. Rather

The stately *Queen Mary* at the Ocean Terminal. *(Albert Wilhelmi Collection)*

The world's largest liner, the 83,673grt, 1,031ft-long *Queen Elizabeth*, alongside the Ocean Terminal at Southampton. *(Albert Wilhelmi Collection)*

The Ocean Dock at Southampton in 1956: the *Queen Elizabeth* is to the left, the laid-up *Scythia* on the right. The latter ship is about to go off to the breakers. *(Albert Wilhelmi Collection)*

New York's Luxury Liner Row in 1957, showing (from top to bottom) the *Independence*, *United States*, *Mauretania*, *Queen Elizabeth* and *Media*. (*James McNamara Collection*)

The splendid all-green, 34,100grt *Caronia* at anchor at Andalsnes, Norway, during a summertime North Cape cruise. (*Cronican-Arroyo Collection*)

unique to Cunard, these cruises ended at Southampton but included in the fare was a first-class return to New York in any Cunarder, including one of the prestigious Queens.

'The *Britannic* had some of the most beautiful public rooms of all Cunarders in the '50s,' remembered the late Willy Smith, a lounge steward. 'There were beautiful, perfectly polished woods and columned lounges with big sofas and enormous soft chairs. There were actual fireplaces and crystal-glass ceiling lamps and magnificent carpets. Some of the carpets came from the great *Aquitania* from before the War.'

John Ferguson, employed at Cunard's grand offices in Lower Manhattan in the 1950s, added:

The *Britannic* would remain at Pier 92, along the Upper West Side, for 6 days. She usually arrived on Saturdays and then sailed again on Fridays. All of the Irish relatives used to greet the *Britannic* as she docked and even if it was late at night. I recall one arrival when she was delayed, arriving at seven in the evening and the passengers not fully cleared until midnight.

It wasn't all glamour and high shipboard comfort after the dark days of the Second World War. Cunard, for example, postponed the decommissioning of the thirty-one-year-old *Aquitania* by war's end, in the summer of 1945. It was later decided that the 45,600-ton ship would run a one-class austerity service between Southampton and Halifax. She was not, of course, restored to her luxurious self this time around. 'Cunard's regular luxury liners were so overbooked in 1949 that we could only get passage back on England on board the *Aquitania*,' remembered the late Betty Green:

The mighty *Queen ELizabeth* making an afternoon arrival at New York in the early 1960s. (*Albert Wilihelmi Collection*)

Cruising comfort: the charming main lounge on board the *Caronia*. *(Albert Wilhelmi Collection)*

Splendour at sea: the vast magnificence of the first-class main lounge aboard the *Queen Mary*. *(Albert Wilhelmi Collection)*

We were in New York [having gone over from Liverpool on the *Britannic*] on a business trip and so had to make the long train journey up to Halifax via Boston. We stayed overnight at the Lord Nelson Hotel in Halifax and could see the four, tall smokestacks from our bedroom window. The *Aquitania* was berthed just across from the hotel, at Pier 21. We sailed at midnight on the following day. The ship was so crowded, almost over-crowded, that some passengers slept in hammocks located in lower-deck dormitories that were left over from the war. My husband and I were allocated to different cabins – he slept in a six-berth cabin, I was in a four-berth stateroom with three other ladies. The ship was still in almost wartime mode. There was little luxury. We did have English stewardesses, however. Baths and toilets were down the corridors and you needed to make a reservation for a 15-minute bath. There was no entertainment other than showing of films in the ship's cinema and occasional dancing in the old ballroom. On milder nights, we had dancing on the outer, upper decks. There was little choice on the daily menus, but the food was still better than the continuing rations back in England.

In December 1949, after an impressive career of thirty-five years, steaming 3 million miles and serving in two world wars, the *Aquitania* was retired. Worn-out and structurally weakened, she was sold to ship-breakers at Faslane in Scotland. It was the end of what was then the last four-stacker and of the great floating palaces from before the First World War.

Another veteran Cunarder, the twenty-five-year-old *Franconia*, was back on the Atlantic run. Richard Gibson served aboard her and remembered:

She was still a beautiful ship, but an old ship. By the 1950s, she was also a tired ship. In post-war, she still had her Queen Anne furniture and the dome over her dining room.

In the first class restaurant, there were still silver napkin rings and damask table cloths and a gallery at the far end for an orchestra. She also had the most beautiful, brass-filled wheelhouse and exceptional deck plank decking.

Gibson added:

In those years, in the late 1940s and '50s, ships such as the *Franconia* actually had three sources of revenue: passengers, cargo and mail. She carried as many as 3,000 bags of mail per crossing and for these the British Government paid Cunard £1.10 for each bag. Among the passengers, we had several guaranteed travellers. Westbound, we carried full loads of immigrants, most of them bound for new homes and lives in Canada. Eastbound, going on specially routed trips to Rotterdam, we had large groups of Canadian NATO forces.

Cunard added four new liners – the *Saxonia*, *Ivernia*, *Carinthia* and *Sylvania* – in 1954–57, primarily for its Canadian services. They would prove, in fact, to be the company's final pure Atlantic passenger ships. One pair sailed from Liverpool, the others from London. 'These Cunarders and many other ships and many different lines and most of them British-flagged at the time used the Port of London,' remembered P.J. Branch, an engineer with the local Port Authority:

In the '50s, the London docks were not just crowded, but jammed with ships. And there was a terrific lot of cranes to work the ships as well as a huge fleet of tugs, barges and all sorts of working craft. There were so many barges that we could walk across them from one side to the dock of the other. Berths were at a premium and ships sometimes remained alongside for as long as two and three weeks. Some vessels actually had to lay

The magnificent *Queen Mary* arriving at New York in a view from October 1949. *(Moran Towing & Transportation Co.)*

The elegant *Queen Mary* pauses overnight at New York's Pier 92 in her final season of service in 1967. *(Cronican-Arroyo Collection)*

off at Southend just waiting for an open berth. And some companies did not like Friday sailings. They were superstitious. You could see all the different funnels above the sheds – British India, P&O, Orient Line, Cunard, Royal Mail, Harrison, Canadian Pacific and Blue Star – and all the companies had their own sheds. The big liners used the Tilbury Landing Stage for the arrivals and outbound embarkations of passengers and then went up to the Royals [named *Albert*, *Victoria* and *King George V*] for cargo-handling and provisioning. Special passenger trains travelled between London's Fenchurch St Station and Tilbury. Otherwise, passengers used taxis directly into the Royal Docks for smaller passenger ships. I recall seeing any number of passenger ships berthed together in the Royals, ships such as the *Dominion Monarch*, *Ivernia*, *Kenya*, *Highland Monarch*, *Rhodesia Castle* and the *Canton*. It was a great sight. But the docks began to fall apart, mostly from industrial troubles and all too many strikes, in the 1960s. By the '70s, they were all but finished. Soon, there was only the odd ship in the docks. An era had passed. It was all very sad, tragic even …

Ships, including passenger liners, were often delayed at London. Fog was the biggest problem back in the 1950s. Many ships would wait at the dock or off Southend. For the ships at anchor, you would hear whistles and fog horns all night long, and on dark, murky November days. Even on the docks themselves, the fog was very thick. It once took me a half-hour to my find bike in the fog. The Clean Air Act of the '60s cured fogs, however, and in just a couple of years.

Sparking competition on the run to Quebec City and Montreal, Canadian Pacific added two new liners, the 25,500-ton *Empress of Britain* and *Empress of England*, in 1956–57. Modern ships, carrying some 1,050 passengers each, the *Empress of Britain* ranked as Britain's first fully air-conditioned liner. 'Ships such as these Empress liners were very good, very solid ships,' remembered one London shipowner. 'They were built especially for the Atlantic. They were strong and sturdy. Comparatively, they were much superior to modern cruise ships in many ways.'

The competition even between British shipping lines was often keen. Historically, the North Atlantic was no exception. 'Cunard's chief competitor on the North Atlantic passenger run to Canada was the Canadian Pacific Company,' recalled Richard Gibson, who sailed as a crew-member on the Cunarders.

There was always fierce competition in early April, just as the winter ice in the St Lawrence River was broken. It was a well-known honour to be the first liner into Quebec City. Once, I recall that our ship, the *Franconia*, was racing with Canadian Pacific's *Empress of France*. It wasn't easy. There was always lots of crunch ice for those final 2 days in the St Lawrence.

Perils at sea did not exclude British passenger ships during the 1950s and '60s. Richard Gibson was on the docking bridge of Cunard's *Franconia* during a voyage in July 1950 when the 20,100-ton liner went aground. He remembered:

The St Lawrence River is very fast-running and, as we were sailing from Quebec City, the pilot made an error near the Isle of Orleans. Quite simply, he miscalculated. We were hard aground, stuck from the bow to the bridge and canted over five degrees. With over 800 passengers on board, we had to work around-the-clock to evacuate the ship. The passengers had to be taken ashore in our lifeboats since the local harbour ferries refused, fearing that the ship would capsize. It was all very orderly and everyone was later sent to local hotels. Their luggage was left behind, however, and was later packed by our staff, using sacks and even blankets. It was brought ashore, but since many passengers were sharing cabins, it then had to be sorted. In the end, however, only two pairs of shoes were missing!

'The *Franconia* was later carefully refloated,' added Gibson:

Tugs had to come from Halifax and later 'see-sawed' the ship off the rocks. She was then pumped out. But she had to miss 2 months of Cunard sailings. She had to spend two months at the Lauzon Dockyard at Quebec City for repairs. It was then the largest local repair job given to a passenger liner. Coincidentally, a year or so later, another Cunarder, the *Samaria*, also grounded in the St Lawrence and also had to be repaired at Lauzon.

Expectedly, there were also some serious accidents, even a few losses. Royal Mail's new 17,500-ton *Magdalena* was wrecked, on her maiden voyage no less, in April 1949 at Rio de Janeiro. Canadian Pacific's *Empress of Canada* burned out and then capsized at her Liverpool berth in January 1953. The 14,600-ton troopship *Empire Windrush*, the former German liner *Monte Rosa* of 1931, burned and then sank in the Mediterranean in March 1954. Booth Line's 7,700grt *Hildebrand* was stranded along the Portuguese coast in September 1957. There were also some close calls. There were some worrisome moments with the 27,600-ton *Oronsay* as she was fitting out at the Vickers yard at Barrow-in-Furness in October 1950. 'The fire was actually quite serious. It started at two in the morning,' recalled Terry Johnson, a shipyard worker at Barrow. 'There was a great struggle with the firefighting hoses and the brand new ship might have been lost. That would have been a great tragedy.'

British shipyards were booming in the late 1940s and '50s, and their virtual production lines of ships included many passenger ships. In the wake of the loss of their *Monarch of Bermuda* while undergoing her post-war refit in 1947, the Furness-Bermuda Line added 440-passenger, all-first-class cruise ship *Ocean Monarch* in 1951. Blue Star opted for a quartet of sixty all-first-class passenger-combo ships, the *Argentina Star*, *Brasil Star*, *Paraguay Star* and *Uruguay Star*, completed in the late 1940s for the London–east coast of South America run. Alternately, to the west coast of the South American continent, Pacific Steam Navigation commissioned the splendid 20,300-ton *Reina Del Mar* in 1956. As determined by her trade, she was fashioned as a three-class ship – a concept of classification then rapidly disappearing. For its rather 'exotic' service from Liverpool to Brazil and 1,000 miles along the Amazon River to Manaus, the Booth Line added two new combo ships, the 7,700grt *Hildebrand* and a slightly larger version, the 8,000grt *Hubert*. On a slightly less exotic run to the Caribbean islands, the Elders & Fyffes Company added two 100-passenger 'banana boats', the *Golfito* and *Camito*.

Union-Castle strengthened its African services with its largest finest mail-ships yet: the 28,700-ton sisters *Edinburgh Castle* and *Pretoria Castle*, added in 1947–48, and

The combination passenger-cargo *Parthia* arrives at New York for the first time in a photograph dating from April 1948. *(Cunard Line)*

Demoded after the Second World War with only a single funnel, the *Georgic* was used during high summer on Cunard's Atlantic service, carrying budget passengers as well as immigrants. *(Albert Wilhelmi Collection)*

Transatlantic retreat: the charming little cocktail bar aboard the all-first-class *Parthia. (Richard Faber Collection)*

Right The 21,900grt *Saxonia*, the first of a new Cunard foursome, arrives at New York for the first time on 6 December 1954. *(Cronican-Arroyo Collection)*

The imposing *Empress of Scotland* carefully departing from New York's Pier 95 on 27 March 1955 during a local tugboat strike. *(Cronican-Arroyo Collection)*

A popular on-board location: the first-class cocktail bar aboard the *Empress of Scotland*. *(Richard Faber Collection)*

Right, from top

In ruins, the fire-gutted, capsized *Empress of Canada* at Liverpool's Gladstone Dock in a view dated January 1953. Her sistership, the *Empress of France*, is berthed just behind. *(Cronican-Arroyo Collection)*

The new 25,500grt, 1,048-passenger *Empress of Britain*'s maiden arrival into Montreal in April 1956. *(Albert Wilhelmi Collection)*

After a ten-day delivery voyage from London, the 516ft-long *Ocean Monarch* arrives in
New York for the first time on 27 April 1951. *(Cronican-Arroyo Collection)*

CUNARD LINE

Liverpool, New York, Boston via Queenstown

A pre-First World War Cunard poster for their Canadian passenger service. *(Author's Collection)*

An effective poster of the *Mauretania* that deliberately enlarges the size of the Cunard liner. *(Author's Collection)*

CUNARD LINE.

First Class Smoking Room. R.M.S. Aquitania. Britains Largest Liner.

WHITE STAR LINE R.M.S. "OLYMPIC"
COMPARED WITH VARIOUS FAMOUS BUILDINGS.

Above, from top
The first-class main lounge aboard the *Lusitania*. *(Richard Faber Collection)*

The first-class smoking room on the *Aquitania*. *(Richard Faber Collection)*

A comparison of the world's great structures by 1911 showing the 882ft-long *Olympic* as being taller than the 790ft-high Woolworth Building in New York, completed in 1913 as the world's biggest skyscraper. *(Richard Faber Collection)*

WHITE STAR   LMS
The Big Ship Route   *The Best Way*
★ BY SEA ★   BY LAND

LMS rail services from London to the Southampton Docks was a convenience offered to passengers sailing on the big White Star liners. *(Author's Collection)*

Don Stoltenberg's painting of the four-funnel *Olympic*. *(Don Stoltenberg Collection)*

American artist Don Stoltenberg's salute to the *Mauretania* in a painting created in 1999. *(Don Stoltenberg Collection)*

Another of Don Stoltenberg's superb paintings, this one dating from 2000 and of the *Aquitania* at Southampton. *(Don Stoltenberg Collection)*

WHITE STAR LINE

SERVICES TO ALL PARTS OF THE WORLD

A White Star Line poster heralding the arrival of the new super-liners *Olympic* and *Titanic* in 1911–12. *(Author's Collection)*

WHITE STAR LINE

R.M.S."OLYMPIC" 46,359 TONS. (THE LARGEST BRITISH STEAMER) VIEWED FROM A SEAPLANE.

SOUTHAMPTON — CHERBOURG — NEW YORK.
LIVERPOOL VIA QUEENSTOWN TO NEW YORK & BOSTON.
LIVERPOOL TO QUEBEC, MONTREAL, HALIFAX & PORTLAND.
ITALY, GIBRALTAR, AZORES, BOSTON & NEW YORK.

For Tickets and all information apply to:—
CURTIS & SON, 156 and 158, Old Christchurch Road, BOURNEMOUTH.

White Star Line used an aerial view of the troopship *Olympic*, done in wartime 'dazzle paint', as a reminder of her heroic service. *(Albert Wilhelmi Collection)*

SOUTHAMPTON

GREAT BRITAIN'S PREMIER DOCKS
owned and managed by the
SOUTHERN RAILWAY OF ENGLAND
For all information, write Docks Manager, Southampton, England.

The giant *Majestic* resting in Southampton's big floating dock was used to promote the port's premier facilities in the 1920s. *(Author's Collection)*

An unusual colour postcard view from the 1920s of the *Berengaria*. *(Albert Wilhelmi Collection)*

Cunard's *Samaria*, one of the company's classic single-stackers of the 1920s. *(Author's Collection)*

ANCHOR LINE TO NEW YORK

A poster advertising Anchor Line passenger services between Glasgow and New York. The forty-seven-story Singer Building is shown on the right. *(Author's Collection)*

A most impressive poster by noted artist Kenneth Shoesmith for Royal Mail's liner service to South America in the 1930s. The view highlights the refitted *Alcantara* and her sister, the *Asturias*. *(Author's Collection)*

A poster from 1930 depicting the Nelson Line service between London and the east coast of South America. *(Author's Collection)*

ABERDEEN & COMMONWEALTH LINE
THE FASTEST LINE TO AUSTRALIA

ONE CLASS SERVICE VIA SUEZ CANAL & COLOMBO

SOUTH & EAST AFRICA
MADEIRA & CANARIES FAST MAIL SERVICE
UNION-CASTLE LINE
Head Office:– 3 Fenchurch St., London, E.C.3.

Aberdeen & Commonwealth Line's inexpensive one-class service between the UK and Australia was popular. *(Author's Collection)*

Out to South and East Africa on board the *Carnarvon Castle* and her sisters, the crack ships in the late 1920s for the Union-Castle Line. *(Author's Collection)*

THE BLUE FUNNEL LINE

TO CANARY I?
SOUTH AFRICA
AUSTRALIA EGYPT
COLOMBO STRAITS
CHINA & JAPAN

KENNETH D SHOESMITH

ALFRED HOLT & CO., India Buildings LIVERPOOL

CANADIAN PACIFIC

TO CANADA-U.S.A.

The *Empress of Japan* is highlighted in this poster commemorating Canadian Pacific's trans-Pacific liner service in the 1930s. *(Author's Collection)*

Liverpool-based Blue Funnel Line traded to the Far East and South East Asia as well to Australia. *(Author's Collection)*

"THE EMPRESS OF BRITAIN READY TO LEAVE SOUTHAMPTON DOCKS FOR CANADA"

SOUTHAMPTON DOCKS
THE GATEWAY TO THE WORLD
Owned and Managed by the Southern Railway.

The great *Empress of Britain* is seen
in this promotional view of the vast
Southampton Docks of the 1930s.
(Author's Collection)

A view celebrating the first year of the record-breaking *Queen Mary*. She is depicted steaming on, however, while in New York harbour. *(Author's Collection)*

Artist Donald Stoltenberg's commemorative of the great *Queen Mary*. The painting dates from 1998. *(Don Stoltenberg Collection)*

R.M.S. "Queen Mary"—Britain's Masterpiece
as she would appear if placed across Trafalgar Square, London.

Cunard White Star

A fascinating comparison: the 81,200grt *Queen Mary* as if placed in London's Trafalgar Square. *(Albert Wilhelmi Collection)*

Artist Rhys Williams celebrated 'the largest ships to London', P&O's *Strathnaver* and *Strathaird*, in 1931–32. *(Albert Wilhelmi Collection)*

A poster depicting the new White Star liners *Britannic* and *Georgic*, said to be the largest motor-liners in the world in the early 1930s. *(Author's Collection)*

Bon voyage: a spirited sailing of the *Queen of Bermuda* from New York's Pier 95. The view dates from 1955. *(Author's Collection)*

Artist Don Stoltenberg's painting of the *Queen of Bermuda* in a work dating from 1998. *(Don Stoltenberg Collection)*

Done in all-white for tropical cruising, the *Mauretania* often sailed on 'bargain cruises' in her final years. *(Author's Collection)*

CUNARD
U·S·A·CANADA

A Cunard poster dating from the late 1930s and promoting their North Atlantic liner services. *(Author's Collection)*

HOMERIC
WEST INDIES

THE CRUISING SHIP OF SPLENDOUR
★ 35,000 TONS ★
40 DAYS FROM 80 GNS
WHITE STAR LINE

In the 1930s, the Orient Line offered summertime cruises to Norway and the northern cities as well as to the Mediterranean and Atlantic isles. *(Author's Collection)*

White Star Line cruises in the early 1930s included a forty-night voyage on board the *Homeric*. *(Author's Collection)*

ORIENT LINE
CRUISES

Managers: ANDERSON GREEN & Cº Lᵀᴰ 5, FENCHURCH AVENUE. LONDON.E.C.3.

A trip on Liverpool's overhead railway offered fine views out over the Mersey of ships and especially of the great liners. The railway was, quite sadly, demolished in the early 1950s. *(Author's Collection)*

Already painted in wartime grey, the *Queen Mary* waits at New York's Pier 90 in September 1939. The *Normandie*'s bow is to the left and the *Aquitania* on the right. *(Author's Collection)*

New York's 'Luxury Liner Row' in September 1939 with (from top to bottom) the *Conte di Savoia*, *Aquitania*, *Queen Mary*, *Normandie* and *Ile de France* at berth. *(Author's Collection)*

R.M.S. Queen Elizabeth

Artist Don Stoltenberg's great tribute to the very great *Queen Elizabeth* in a painting done in 1999. *(Donald Stoltenberg Collection)*

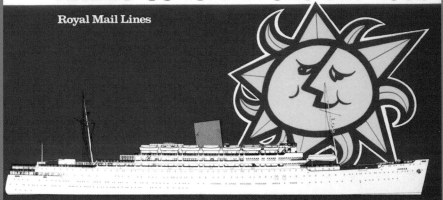

ANDES SUNSHINE CRUISES 1966

Royal Mail Lines

A brochure cover from the mid-1960s for the very popular *Andes* of Royal Mail Lines. *(Author's Collection)*

A fine colour rendering of the classic *Queen of Bermuda* with Hamilton in the background. *(Author's Collection)*

TWO DAYS *from New York!...the pleasure planned liner, Queen of Bermuda, enters her home port, Bermuda*

Cunard souvenirs: a box of matches from the *Queen Elizabeth* in the 1950s. *(Author's Collection)*

The cover of an elaborate brochure made for the *Caronia*'s summertime North Cape cruise in 1961. *(Author's Collection)*

EUROPE
U.S.A.
CANADA

CUNARD

45 days 23 ports 13,000 miles 11 countries

CUNARD LINE

NORTH CAPE CRUISE

SAILING FROM NEW YORK   JUNE 30, 1960

CUNARD'S FAMOUS WORLD CRUISE LINER CARONIA

SHIP and TRAVEL by B.I.

A HUNDRED YEARS OF SERVICE 1856 TO 1956

BRITISH INDIA STEAM NAVIGATION COMPANY LIMITED

A poster celebrating 100 years of British India Line services. *(Author's Collection)*

Down Under: a P&O poster highlighting the company's diverse and varied passenger ship itineraries. *(Author's Collection)*

In December 1967 the thirty-one-year-old *Queen Mary* arrived in Long Beach, California, to begin her conversion to a moored hotel, museum and collection of shops and restaurants. *(Queen Mary Hotel)*

The lighted *Queen Mary* reflects across the harbour at Long Beach. This scene dates from the mid-1970s. *(Queen Mary Hotel)*

Some cosmetic changes: The *QE2* undergoes a refit in New York Harbour at the graving dock at Bayonne, New Jersey, in a view dated 10 January 1977. *(Author's Collection)*

Workmen refresh the Cunard name along the 963ft-long liner's starboard side. *(Author's Collection)*

The iconic *QE2* passes another icon, the World Trade Center towers, in a view dating from 1995. *(Richard Faber Collection)*

Another of artist Don Stoltenberg's very fine tributes to the great liners. *(Donald Stoltenberg Collection)*

The smoking-room bar aboard the 440-passenger *Ocean Monarch*. *(Furness-Bermuda Line)*

The splendid Royal Mail Line's flagship *Andes* arriving at Santos, Brazil, in July 1953. *(Laire Jose Giraud Collection)*

then a trio of 526 berth, all-cabin-class, 17,000-tonners for its extensive round-Africa service. These were named *Rhodesia Castle*, *Braemar Castle* and *Kenya Castle*, added in 1951–52. Union-Castle also experimented with a one-class migrant-style ship, the 18,400-ton *Bloemfontein Castle*, in 1950. Largely unsuccessful, she was sold off in nine years. On the West African run, Elder Dempster commissioned the 11,600grt sisters *Accra* and *Apapa* in 1947–48 and then a larger improved version, the Company flagship, the 14,000grt *Aureol*, in 1951.

Ellerman Lines added four combo ships, the 107-passenger *City of Port Elizabeth*, *City of Exeter*, *City of York* and *City of Durban*, between 1952 and 1954. Used on the London–South & East Africa trade, they were extremely well run and likened to being 'big yachts'. Meanwhile, British India strengthened its colonial run from London to East Africa with two near-sisters, the 14,400-ton *Kenya* and the *Uganda*, in 1951–52. They also added no less than ten other post-war passenger ships, ranging from the likes of the 5,000-ton *Dara* to the 10,300-ton *Karanja* and *Kampala* for their passenger services based at Bombay and Calcutta, and which never touched British ports.

The Australian liner trade boomed by the 1950s, both with regular passenger traffic and with the outbound, ten fare-assisted migrant trade. In peak times as many as 100,000 Britons were heading for 'better lives and better jobs', as one Manchester family noted, in that 'far off paradise' Down Under. The Orient Line had some of the very finest British liners on the Aussie run. Their post-war rebuilding programme included the 28,100-ton *Orcades*, added in 1948; the 27,900-ton *Oronsay* of 1951; and the 28,800-ton *Orsova* of 1954. Howard Franklin often sailed aboard the Orient Line passenger ships in the 1960s and recalled the *Orcades*, *Oronsay* and *Orsova*. 'Orient Line was a very British company, both in style and tone. The officers had distinctive uniforms with high neck collars and that were very clean cut. They looked very, very British,' he remembered:

> Travelling in Orient Line was a cross between a grand hotel and an English public school. It was all very orderly. In first-class, there was superb service, highlighted by the Silver Grills for select dining. It was very French-designed food and all the menus were in French as well. Orient Line was quite different from P&O. Both were utterly British, but the Orient Line was still very colonial. There were huge numbers of both the British Army and Indian Army on board plus Indian maharajas with their wives and entourages. The Orient Line interiors were very comfortable, but minimalist. They were very 1950s. There was, as I recall, lots of use of mosaics and lino flooring.

P&O's post-war rebuilding programme included the 27,900-ton *Himalaya* of 1949, the 24,200-ton *Chusan* of 1950 and then, biggest of all, the 29,700grt near-sisters *Arcadia* and *Iberia*, added in 1954. The 1,026-passenger *Chusan* was created, it must be noted, for the London Suez Bombay Far East service. 'P&O had some of the finest liners under the British flag,' said Howard Franklin, a long-time passenger and frequent guest lecturer aboard the great P&O Lines – one of the most illustrious shipping lines and still sailing today but as Carnival Corporation-owned P&O Cruises. In earlier days, up until the 1970s, P&O Lines was mostly interested, however, in long-haul two-class passenger ship services, usually between Britain and Australia, but to other parts of the world as well. Their liners touched on over 100 ports in all.

In the King George V Dock at London, the brand-new *Magdalena* prepares for her maiden voyage to South America. She was built to especially replace the *Highland Patriot* which was lost during the war. Unfortunately, the *Magdalena* herself was soon lost, being wrecked near Rio de Janeiro. *(Cronican-Arroyo Collection)*

A first-class double-bedded cabin aboard Blue Star Line's *Brasil Star*, a ship completed in 1948. *(Richard Faber Collection)*

P&O's mainline operation was from London to Sydney via the Suez route. The itineraries usually included Gibraltar, Marseilles, Port Said, Aden, Colombo, Fremantle and then Melbourne. Business boomed for passengers as well as some high-grade freight and the all-important mails, and so newer bigger ships were the order of the day. Trading was also heavily sparked by a brisk business with mostly post-war British immigrants, including full families who were then seeking new lives in opportunity-rich Australia. 'Life Down Under' seemed to be like a paradise. In some years, in the 1950s and into the 1960s, as many as 100,000 Brits headed for Australian shores and new lives. That vast continent beckoned as so-called 'New Australia'.

'They were all wonderful ships, but for me, the *Arcadia* had something special about her,' remembered Howard Franklin:

She had the most wonderful library with club chairs. You could just curl-up and read a good book. P&O ships differed from their close rivals, the big liners of the Orient Line, which was also British. P&O was more egalitarian. There was less aristocracy in first class, for example. Orient Line ships felt like big country houses gone to sea while P&O liners were more hotels at sea. Orient Line also had better food and impeccable service in first class, which was superior to P&O.

Slightly smaller, the 24,000-ton *Chusan*, commissioned in 1950, was actually designed for another secondary P&O service, the classic Far Eastern run – from London via Suez to Bombay, Singapore, Hong Kong, Kobe and Yokohama. This was the Far East Run. 'At P&O in those days, the *Chusan* was said to be the absolute best ship in the fleet – the best built, the friendliest, the best run,' added Franklin.

'P&O had a great reputation in Australia in the 1950s. Their ships were, as I remember, slightly more popular, even more beloved, to Australians. They were known as "white ships with gold funnels". Myself, I loved them all, but especially the *Himalaya*,' remembered Clifford Hocking, an avid Australian ocean-liner enthusiast and traveller.

P&O had special touches. They served candied fruit at dinner whereas the rival Orient Line did not. P&O had wonderful Indian service. It was part of a lost age, it seemed, even in the '50s. There was the ritual of beef tea and a dry biscuit at 11 each morning. Otherwise, life on board was quite simple. You'd sit around all day and either talk to yourself or torture someone else. There were still strict barriers between classes and, to cross, you'd have to jump half door partitions. The long voyages between London and Australia included immigrants and there were Italians and Greeks on board as well as Brits and Aussies. There was also the first class business trade. On P&O liners, there were two different worlds between first class and tourist class. Their liners also carried lots of cargo and mail.

'We had lots of liners at Melbourne in the '50s,' added Clifford Hocking. 'I'd go down to Station Pier once or twice a week just to see them. We'd also go down to see family and friends off. There were railway lines direct into the pier. Departures were huge events. There were masses of streamers and very tearful goodbyes.'

'I well remember the great excitement of sailing day at London (and later Southampton) on the P&O and Orient liners,' commented Howard Franklin. 'There were reunions, meetings, that sense of settling in aboard a big liner. I also remember seeing the commodore of the Orient Line. He was a very precise man, very exacting.'

P&O passenger ships were well known for their Indian crews, especially the Goanese in the passenger areas. 'There was a Head Sherang [liason], who hired all the Indian crews. They were like sergeant majors in the British Army,' said the late Len Wilton, formerly of P&O's passenger division in London:

When a liner was new, hundreds of Indians used to arrive at the shipyard for the first voyages. I recall them boarding the brand new *Himalaya*, *Chusan*, *Arcadia* and *Iberia*. On board, they were akin to a separate community amongst the crew and had their own Indian galleys. There was great tradition among them. They had worked from father to son and often beginning with grandfather. Indian crews were also aboard Ellerman and British India passenger ships. Of course, on board passenger ships, it was a better standard of living than home. Some sailed for 40 and even 50 years. Head offices actually preferred them. They were clean, friendly and well spoken. They preferred British shipping lines than compared to, say, the Greeks, who would scream and yell at him.

'There were some larger-than-life characters amongst the European crew on the P&O and Orient liners,' added Howard Franklin. 'There were waiters and bedroom stewards that were much like entertainers. Shipboard was their stage and the passengers their audiences.'

Long-haul passenger ships, for example on the Australian, East African and Indian routes to and from the UK, also offered mini-voyages that appealed to many passenger-ship enthusiasts. Leslie Shaw recalled such short voyages in the 1950s on the likes of the homeward-bound *Strathaird* and *Stratheden* of P&O, the *Orontes* and *Otranto* of the Orient Line and even the *Uganda* of British India:

There were always available berths from Marseilles to London as many of the homebound passengers wanted to eliminate the passage in the notorious Bay of Biscay and also to save time. They would leave the ship at the French port, train to the English Channel and then cross by Channel ferry for the last leg of their journey. We did the reverse: the Dover to Calais ferry, then by train to Paris, where we often spent the day, and then made the daylight train run from the French capital to Nice. We then joined the next homeward liner, which often also called at Gibraltar en route. Of course, for speed, the connection between London and Nice could be made in 24 hours. There was always two lots of passengers aboard the ships coming home from Sydney, Melbourne & Fremantle. They were earlier migrants. Some were successful and loved Australia and others were unsuccessful and hated it. The successful were revisiting Britain & Europe for family trips or as tourists; the unsuccessful were returning to resettle in Britain. There were also always a dozen or so British Army officers in first class and the sergeants and lower ranks in tourist class. I remember these officers marching about the upper decks in great style.

'Older, smaller immigrant ships took as much as six and eight weeks to sail one-way from the UK to Australia in the 1950s,' recalled P.J. Branch:

South to the sun! The twin-funnel *Arundel Castle* berthed at Cape Town with famed Table Mountain in the background. *(Albert Wilhelmi Collection)*

British India's *Uganda* departs from Marseilles as part of her voyages between London, the Suez and East Africa. *(Albert Wilhelmi Collection)*

Flagship to West Africa: Elder Dempster Line's smart-looking *Aureol* waits at anchor in the River Mersey at Liverpool. *(F. Leonard Jackson Collection)*

Used in the extensive round Africa service, the 552-berth, all-cabin-class *Braemar Castle* calls at Cape Town. *(Robert Pabst Collection)*

The fine-looking *Orcades*, commissioned in 1948, departs from Sydney. *(Albert Wilhelmi Collection)*

The first-class reading and writing room aboard P&O's *Himalaya* of 1949. *(Richard Faber Collection)*

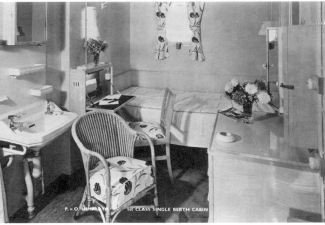

A first-class single cabin, complete with private shower and toilet, aboard the *Himalaya*. *(Richard Faber Collection)*

Fire at the shipyard: the incomplete *Oronsay* is damaged by a fire at the Vickers' yard at Barrow in the autumn of 1950. *(Albert Wilhelmi Collection)*

Requiring approval from the Australian Government's offices in London, British migrants were offered a £10 fare [approximately $40] and in a time when a week's wages were $45. Everyone was required to stay a minimum of two years. It was quite successful. Most stayed and built generally happy and successful lives Down Under. But later, some couples worked two and three jobs to earn the passage monies to come home and also to repay the Australian Government. Australia was not everyone's paradise …

Many of the older migrant ships – which included ships as the *Chitral*, *Ranchi*, *Georgic*, *Asturias* and *New Australia* – were actually passed their best. I remember the old *Esperance Bay*. She was leaking all over the place. With a green-coloured hull, she was known to us and less than affectionately as the 'green devil'.

When Queen Elizabeth II named the 20,000-ton *Southern Cross* at her launching in August 1954, the ship attracted great attention. She was the Shaw Savill Line's first big liner since their *Dominion Monarch* of 1939 and, of course, was notable in being yet another liner built by the famed Harland & Wolff Co. at Belfast. But more importantly, the 604ft-long *Southern Cross* was a totally different passenger ship, one created as the result of extensive research. She was, for example, the first large liner, British or otherwise, to have her funnel mounted aft and therefore freeing the midships section for passenger areas, pools and open-air sections. This was soon copied by many other passenger-ship designers. Secondly, she was also the first all-tourist-class liner, carrying 1,100 at full capacity and in cabins from upper-deck singles to economical four- and six-berth rooms on her lower decks. There were no class divisions on board the *Southern Cross*; Passengers had the full run of the ship. Furthermore, she was the first pure passenger liner that carried no cargo whatsoever other than baggage and some mail. Finally, unlike all other British liners servicing Australia, the 20-knot *Southern Cross* was routed on continuous ten-week trips around the world – from Southampton to South Africa, then across to Australia, then northward to Panama and the Caribbean before returning to the UK or, on occasion, the itinerary was done in reverse. A very popular ship from the start, she carried British immigrants to Australia, budget Australians going to Britain and Europe on extended vacations and the occasional tourist, some of whom actually made the entire world voyage as a sort of cruise. She was so successful that a near-sister, the somewhat larger *Northern Star*, was added to the Shaw Savill fleet in 1962.

'We carried many, many immigrants on board the *Southern Cross*, even well into the 1960s,' recalled Jim Clench, an engineer with Shaw Savill:

In the '50s and '60s, many British people were seeking a better life elsewhere and went to Australia House in London to apply for a fare-assisted passage Down Under. They then waited. It was, after all, a £10 fare for the entire four-week voyage from Southampton to Fremantle, Melbourne or Sydney. At the time, many people in the UK saw Australia as a palm tree-lined paradise. They did not see the harsh reality …

An orchestra was the only entertainment on board the *Southern Cross* … There was also a small jazz band in the ship's pub-bar and a disco girl for records. The purser also served as the cruise director. Few cabins had private facilities and there were two dining rooms with two sittings at each meal. The British migrants going to Australia were often impatient at meal times, however. Some had never been served by a waiter in their lives and often were quite rude and demanding of the staff. Coming home to Southampton, we would have about 1,000 passengers aboard, about 90% of capacity. There would be returning immigrants, who had done well in Australia, as well as Australian backpackers. They were 'real passengers,' in a better mood, with a different outlook and purpose to their voyage, and they even gave tips to the staff. The crew was in better spirits as well. Of course, we had an all-British crew on board. Basically, Shaw Savill Line was a cargo company that had some passenger ships whereas P&O-Orient, our greatest rival, was a passenger company with some cargo ships.

The original plan for the *Northern Star* was to eliminate a funnel altogether and instead use twin uptakes, similar to those on the *Rotterdam* and the *Canberra*. But some tradition prevailed in the end and the new ship, at 24,000 tons and 650ft in length (and therefore larger than the *Southern Cross*), would have a conventional stack. She was ceremoniously launched by Queen Elizabeth the Queen Mother at the Cammell Laird's yard at Birkenhead in June 1961. It seemed fitting to have a royal launch as Queen Elizabeth II had named the *Southern Cross* seven years earlier, in 1954. The new *Northern Star* was ready for her first seventy-six-night, globe-circling trip in the summer of 1962.

'The *Northern Star* carried 1,400 passengers, 300 more than the *Southern* Cross,' recalled Tony Ralph, who was employed by Shaw Savill in the early 1970s. He served both in the company's headquarters in London's Haymarket and aboard the passenger ships themselves:

The *Northern Star* was also more modern than the *Southern Cross*, quite different in many ways. She had much more formica and lots of linoleum. She was more functional in tone. Actually, she lacked the warmer qualities and overall British passenger ship-tone of the *Southern Cross* …

Unfortunately, the *Northern Star* was not an especially successful ship … She had mechanical problems almost from Day 1. There were breakdowns of all sorts.

In the late 1940s, Shaw Savill had added a quartet of fine 15,000grt combo liners, each carrying eighty-five first-class passengers. They were named *Athenic*, *Corinthic*, *Gothic* and *Ceramic*, and were used on the long-haul London–New Zealand via Panama service. The 564ft-long *Ceramic* was to be used in 1951 for the world tour of King George VI and Queen Elizabeth but the King's worrisome declining health prompted postponements. In the end the *Gothic* was selected for the royal tour, but in the fall of 1954 and for Queen Elizabeth II. The Queen, Prince Philip and their entourage used the ship for months, until May 1954. 'She had a major overhaul and refit in preparation. Harland & Wolff, Silley Weir and many other ship repair firms were involved,' recalled P.J. Branch, an engineer with the Port of London. 'In all, it took 8 weeks to prepare the *Gothic*. Her engines were overhauled, her passenger areas re-carpeted, many of the cabins remodelled and her hull was repainted entirely in white. She was, to a great extent, a large royal yacht.'

Also on the long-distance run to Auckland and Wellington, the New Zealand Shipping Co., which was British-flagged, added two 21,900-ton, very large combo liners, the 416-passenger *Rangitane* and *Rangitoto*, in 1949. A slightly smaller version, the 267-berth *Ruahine* joined the service two years later, in 1951. And for its Liverpool–Australia service, the Blue Funnel Line opted for combo type ships as well, but with far less capacity – the thirty-passenger foursome of *Helenus*, *Jason*, *Hector* and *Ixion*. A second quartet, the 10,000grt *Peleus*, *Pyrrhus*, *Patroclus* and *Perseus*, were built for the company's Liverpool–Far East run.

Trooping by sea was still very much in Government planning in the 1950s and two large troopships were constructed, the 20,500-ton *Nevasa* and 20,600-ton *Oxfordshire*. Chartered to the Ministry of Transport, the ships were owned by the British India and Bibby lines respectively. Troop deployments were, however, shifted entirely to air by 1962.

Not all British passenger ships were large or luxurious or especially well known. Some served on very specific services. Two examples were Blue Funnel Line's *Gorgon* and *Charon*, twin ships built in 1933 and 1936 respectively, and which carried as many as eighty passengers each. They were among the many smaller and now largely forgotten 'workhorses' of the British passenger fleet that endured well into the 1950s and '60s. Dr David Kirkman sailed aboard these otherwise fine, hardworking little ships beginning in the late 1940s and in the 1950s:

They were very simple ships that had flat bottoms. They were really substandard, even after the Second World War. There were sea water showers, which was really just a bucket of water. There were British officers and a Chinese crew, who lived in hammocks that were far aft, just over the propeller. The radio officer actually dubbed as a purser. There were louvered doors on all the cabins and the Chinese stewards never knocked, but ran their fingers along the louvers. They were quite popular on the run between Fremantle and Singapore, but made various stops along the way – at Geralton, Carnarvon, Onslow, Port Hedland, Broome and Derby. They'd pass through the Lombok Strait, between Bali and Java, which was a mile wide. They were scheduled for one-month roundtrips. It was 12 days from Fremantle to Singapore. They would load produce, fruits and vegetables, at Fremantle and then load cattle at Broome and Derby. The ships were registered in Liverpool, to Alfred Holt & Co. Ltd, the parent of the very famous, very well known Blue Funnel Line. But the British officers used to say that if these ships ever returned to Britain, the Board of Trade would never certify them. They also said that they were British flag-by-distance. Almost amazingly, they remained sailed until 1964, and under the British flag to the very end …

The accommodations had forced-air ventilation … They offered leisurely passages that were very popular especially with older Australians. There was little entertainment other than picture shows in the lounge, games and, of course, bingo. It was all one sitting in the restaurant.

Another classic case was British India's 8,500grt *Rajula*, built in 1926 and then certified to carry over 5,000 passengers, sailed until 1975, making for a career of forty-nine years.

Big, fast jet aircraft first crossed the Atlantic in October 1958. The effects, namely the daunting competition, were felt almost immediately even if the likes of Cunard described flying as a 'mere fad'. The passenger ship industry rattled, almost like never before.

Completed in the spring of 1954, the 'mast-less' *Orsova* arriving at the Tilbury Docks in London. *(Luis Miguel Correia Collection)*

The sleek 708ft-long *Oronsay* is seen departing from San Francisco on one of her long-haul around-the-world voyages for P&O Orient Lines. *(Cronican-Arroyo Collection)*

A great favourite in the P&O fleet, the *Arcadia* of 1954 is seen passing through the Suez Canal. *(P&O)*

The *Orsova* is seen passing under the Sydney Harbour Bridge in a view dated December 1964. Captain Craddock can be seen in the wheelhouse window. *(Author's Collection)*

A great aerial view of the Tilbury Docks in 1960. The *Arcadia* is on the left. The *Stratheden*, *Strathnaver* and *Himalaya* are berthed together (from left to right) while the *Strathmore* is above and in dry dock. On the right, at the Tilbury landing stage, is Royal Mail's *Amazon*. *(P&O)*

Pre-war veterans from the 1920s and near sisters, the twin-funneled *Otranto* (*left*) and *Orontes* together at Hobart, Tasmania, in 1955. *(P&O)*

A great combination passenger-cargo liner belonging to the Bibby Line, the 115-passenger *Derbyshire* is being loaded with cargo at Birkenhead prior to another long voyage out to Rangoon. *(F. Leonard Jackson Collection)*

Another very large combination passenger-cargo ship, the 21,800grt *Rangitoto* of 1949 is seen in New Zealand waters. *(Gillespie-Faber Collection)*

After a long and distinguished service, the thirty-year-old *Mooltan* of P&O is towed off to the breakers in Scotland in 1954. *(P&O)*

The Ministry of Transport troopship *Dilwara*, managed by British India Line, is berthed at Southampton with Booth Line's *Hildebrandt* in the background. *(P&O)*

While being used as a royal yacht, the flag-dressed *Gothic* arrives at Valletta, Malta, on 4 May 1954. *(Michael Cassar Collection)*

Hail and farewell: the thirty-year-old *Strathnaver* departs from Sydney for London for the last time in a view from spring 1962. *(Lindsay Johnstone Collection)*

A classic combo ship with up to thirty passenger berths, Blue Funnel's *Perseus* worked the Liverpool–Far East run with three identical sisters. *(Gillespie-Faber Collection)*

Being towed off to Rotterdam to become a shipyard training ship, Anchor Line's 1937-built *Cilicia* is seen in this 1965 view. *(Steffen Weirauch Collection)*

The Greek cruise ship-ferry *Mediterranean Sea*, the former combo ship *City of Exeter* of the Ellerman Lines, is being broken-up in this scene at Aliaga in Turkey, dated July 1999. *(Selim San Collection)*

Further service: two former Union-Castle liners, the ex-*Kenya Castle* on the left and the one-time *Dunnottar Castle* on the right, are together at San Juan, Puerto Rico, in this view, from 1989. By then the two liners were serving as cruise ships for Chandris Lines as the *Amerikanis* and *The Victoria* respectively. A third Chandris cruise ship, *The Azur*, is on the far right. She had been the P&O ferry *Eagle* in her earlier life. (*Luis Miguel Correia Collection*)

As if it was the end of the empire, British India's small 5,000grt *Dwarka* was the last of the company's overseas passenger ships. She served on the India–Persian Gulf and endured until 1982 before going to the breakers. (*P&O*)

The fates of ageing Atlantic liners were sealed soon after those first jet flights across the Atlantic. Cunard's *Britannic* was one example. Thirty years old, she had a massive mechanical breakdown in the spring of 1960 and so had to stay at Pier 90 in New York for months. A local shipyard sensibly handled pier-side repairs. Using floating work barges and cranes, it then ranked as the largest pier-side repair job of its kind. But it cost Cunard millions in lost bookings and cancellations. Months later, and under a moody, dark December sky, the *Britannic* sailed from New York for the very last time. After offloading her final passengers and then de-storing at Liverpool, she headed north to Inverkeithing in Scotland to be broken-up. By then she was the last liner linked to the White Star Line.

The great days of the British passenger-ship business seemed to be in steady decline in the 1960s and into the early 1970s. The big British maritime strike of May–June 1966 was a devastating blow. The entire fleet, passenger ships included, was idle for six weeks. 'Crew costs killed the British merchant navy,' added Len Wilton of P&O. 'British officers were even costly. Shipping companies found it increasingly difficult to make a profit.' Then cargo in passenger ship holds began going over to new, faster, more efficient containerships. And as British liners aged, their insurances escalated and they often needed expensive refits and repairs.

Far-off Taiwan was scrapping countless ships in the 1970s and among them was a near-armada of money-losing, often ageing British liners. Between 1972 and 1976, noted liners such as the *Orcades*, *Oronsay*, *Orsova*, *Himalaya*, *Chusan*, *Iberia*, *Northern Star*, *Reina Del Mar*, *Nevasa*, *S.A. Oranje* (the former *Pretoria Castle*) and the *Edinburgh Castle* all made one-way voyages to the scrapyards of Kaohsiung.

Cunard alone retired eleven passenger ships between 1960 and 1968. Filled with nostalgia, Douglass Campbell made the *Queen Mary*'s final Atlantic crossing from New York to Cherbourg and Southampton in September 1967. He remembered:

By then, there had been a great cut-down in help. There were actually economies everywhere. Cunard was trying to rekindle the bygone style, but it was really lost, very faded glamour. John Roosevelt [the son of Franklin and Eleanor Roosevelt] was the auctioneer for the ship's mileage pool and Walter Lord [author of *A Night to Remember*, among other books] was also aboard. We passed the *Queen Elizabeth* at night and felt very sad. We also thought that the on board model of the *QE2*, then just launched, looked so strange, so different.

Other British passenger routes were not so seriously affected by air competition until the 1960s. East of Suez, on the Australian and Far Eastern routes, was not affected in earnest until the late 1960s, a full decade after the first jets offered full and serious competition on the North Atlantic. 'Even by the '50s, change was coming,' remembered Clifford Hocking, a long-time loyalist to the great P&O liners on the UK–Australian route. 'I flew to England for the first time in April 1954,' he added. 'It was 78 hours from Melbourne to Sydney and then to London by way of Darwin, Calcutta and Beirut. It was quite expensive when compared to the ship, however, and $9,000 roundtrip.'

seven

CHANGING COURSE: NEW COMPETITION

Dubbed the 'last Atlantic super-liner', Her Majesty the Queen named the *Queen Elizabeth 2* at the 65,800-ton ship's launching at Clydebank in September 1967. Cunard was often criticised for building such a vessel for a trade that seemed all but over. She was the last British liner, built in a British shipyard and for British owners. In fact, the 963ft-long *QE2*, as she was almost immediately dubbed, went on to sail for thirty-nine years and created numerous ocean liner records: the longest serving Cunarder, sailing 5.3 million nautical miles (or the equivalent of twelve round trips to the moon), transporting 3 million passengers and visiting her home port of Southampton 651 times. She proved to be, even with some periodic uncertain times, the most successful big liner of all time.

Britain had a final burst, it seems, of building new liners for the early 1960s. It was indeed the last hurrah. Canadian Pacific seeing hope on the Atlantic, for example, added the 27,200-ton *Empress of Canada* in 1961.

Even the UK–South American passenger service trudged on for another decade. Royal Mail Lines was the last to build new tonnage for Latin American liner operations, however. In 1959–60 they added a brand new trio of handsome-looking passenger-cargo liners, the 20,000-ton *Amazon* and her twin sisters, the *Aragon* and *Arlanza*. Capped by single buff-yellow funnels, they were in fact the very last passenger ships in the British fleet to have divided superstructures (the officers being separated from the passenger-guests) and the very last to cater to three classes: first, cabin and third class. They were also the final new British liners to use the term 'third class'. They were, however, somewhat late for the South American passenger run, which was rapidly being overtaken by the airlines in the 1960s, and all the while their cargo operations were complicated by strikes, often in the Port of London. 'They sometimes returned to South America with the same cargo that they brought north on the previous trip. The London dockers had been on yet another long, unhappy strike and refused to unload ships such as these,' remembered the late Ron Peach, a Royal Mail steward. 'Royal Mail was not only beginning to lose patience, but lots of money as well.'

Union-Castle planned no less than three large liners: the 28,600-ton *Pendennis Castle* of 1958, then the 37,600-ton *Windsor Castle* of 1960 (the largest, fastest company liner ever) and finally the 32,700-ton *Transvaal Castle* a year later. 'First class on Union Castle in the 1950s and '60s was very similar to first class on the Orient Line. It was all very formal, very old world, very grand,' remembered Howard Franklin. 'Union-Castle was all full in winter and often full of very formal, sometimes even very stuffy people.

Some families came aboard every year, on the same sailing, at the same table, in the same stateroom. Whole families would be going out to South Africa for 2–3 months for long, winter holidays.'

The P&O and the Orient lines merged as P&O-Orient Lines beginning in 1960, and were the most ambitious of the time, creating the 41,900-ton *Oriana* of 1960 and then, bigger still, the 45,200-ton *Canberra* a year later. They were the biggest, fastest, finest liners ever built for the still busy UK–Australia trade. Inevitably, the two mighty ships were compared. 'First class on board the *Oriana* was quite different from the *Canberra*,' according to Howard Franklin:

The *Oriana* was, it seemed, all graciousness and luxury and lots of carpets whereas the *Canberra* was more informal and acres and acres of lino. The *Oriana* also had a Silver Grill Restaurant, but which, quite sadly, was made over into cabins in later years. Her Monkey Bar and Garden was very popular and made you feel as if you were suspended over the ocean itself. At the Monkey Bart, there were also enormous proportions of drinks!

The handsome-looking *Canberra*, the P&O-Orient flagship which had enormous press coverage in 1961, her maiden year, also had her problems. 'The weight of her machinery, which was placed far aft, was under-estimated by as much as 1,000 tons by Harland & Wolff, her builders,' recalled John Bolton, a marine engineer based at Liverpool:

On her sea trials, she operated like a speedboat. Her bow was practically out of the water. The number one cargo hold had to be filled with ballast so that the head [bow] would be down. When machinery is positioned aft, it can be worrisome with weight. Another liner of that period, the Italian-built *Oceanic*, had a slight problem as well and so was never fully functional. Technically, the *Canberra* was something of a disaster whereas the *Oriana* was far more efficient and operationally successful, but just rather dreadful looking.

'I always felt that the *Canberra* was a darker, even more oppressive ship. She lacked light,' noted Howard Franklin:

Preparing for her maiden voyage in January 1962, the 32,600grt *Transvaal Castle* – the last of the Union-Castle liners – is seen at Southampton. The Atlantic super-liners *United States* and *Queen Mary* are berthed behind. *(Albert Wilhelmi Collection)*

The last Canadian Pacific liner, the 27,200-ton *Empress of Canada*, departs from her builder's yard at Newcastle in February 1961. The bow of the new Portuguese liner *Principe Perfeito* is on the upper right. *(Richard Faber Collection)*

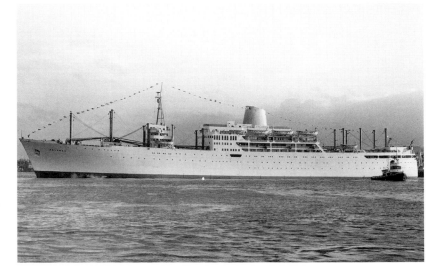

Royal Mail's 20,300grt *Arlanza* and her two sisters were the last liners built for the UK-South America run when they were completed in 1959-60. *(Richard Faber Collection)*

Down the ways: Orient Line's superb 41,900grt *Oriana* is launched at Vickers' yard at Barrow-in-Furness on 3 November 1959. *(P&O)*

Th Oriana – with the smaller *Oronsay* on the left – bethed at Station Pier, Melbourne. *(Lindsay Johnstone Collection)*

Used as a hotel and entertainment centre, the moored *Oriana* is seen here at Shanghai in a photograph dated 21 November 2000. *(Peter Knego Collection)*

Ready to be named and launched, the 45,200grt *Canberra* sits majestically on the ways at Harland & Wolff, Belfast, in a scene dating from March 1960. *(Harland & Wolff Ltd)*

Soon to be named by Her Majesty Queen Elizabeth the Queen Mother at the Cammell Laird shipyard at Birkenhead, the 24,700grt *Northern Star* is seen in this photograph dated 27 June 1961. *(Albert Wilhelmi Collection)*

After thirty-six years of service, the beloved *Canberra* returns from her final cruise. The date is September 1997. *(Author's Collection)*

Right The 650ft-long, 1,412-passenger *Northern Star* was a larger version of the highly successful *Southern Cross*, which was completed in 1955. *(Richard Faber Collection)*

A grand farewell: the incomparable *Queen Mary* departs from New York for the very last time in September 1967. *(Albert Wilhelmi Collection)*

The future: the brand new *QE2* leaves the John Brown yard on the Clyde as shown in this view from November 1968. *(Cunard Line)*

She had the great innovation of the court cabins at P&O, however, and these were very practical. The Century Bar was the best room on the ship in my opinion. It was a sort of secret hideaway. But I was never quite as impressed with the *Canberra*. Most of my preferences and affection went to the *Oriana*. Years later, and especially after her heroic duty in the Falklands War, many people were very sentimental about the *Canberra*.

At first there were plans to build a rather traditional ship (with three classes of passengers) to replace the ageing *Queen Mary*, but then these were reworked to a more apt, twin-class, dual-purpose liner that could sail the Atlantic for about six months of the year and cruise for the rest. 'There were original tenders for a new, large *Queen* as early as 1957–58,' recalled a London-based ship designer:

> I was at Vickers and we were building the *Oriana* [41,000 tons] for the Orient Line. We tried to sell Cunard on a version of the *Oriana*, but slightly larger at 50,000 tons. There was absolutely no need for a 70–80,000-ton Atlantic Cunader at that time. But Cunard seemed insistent and eventually signed with John Brown's on the Clyde.

A marine engineer in the 1950s and '60s once told me:

> In the British shipping and shipbuilding industries, during the 1960s, both Cunard and John Brown were considered to be over-estimated; they were more famous names by then. In shipping, P&O then had the most envied reputation and the Orient Line was second. Third was Union-Castle. Cunard was then not even in the top three.

Douglass Campbell was aboard the *QE2*'s maiden westbound crossing to New York, in May 1969. 'The *QE2* was not completely finished on that first trip, but she was still pleasant,' he recalled:

> She was totally different from what we had come to expect from Cunard and our three dozen crossings on the original Queens. We felt that old *Queen Mary* actually had some features that were better such as the steam room. In time, we learned to appreciate and even like the *QE2*. By the 1990s, the *QE2* was in pretty good shape for her age and then had the best cabins afloat. The staff cuts were evident, but overall there was a valiant effort. Cunard lived on!

As the age of the line voyage and classic passenger ships began its irretrievable decline, there were many appealing reduced fares to attract an increasingly smaller group of ocean travellers. Leslie Shaw decided on a discounted trip around the world:

> We left London on June 10th 1970, in Shaw Savill's *Arawa* [the former *Arlanza* of Royal Mail], and returned three months later, on September 12th. We sailed out via Las Palmas, Cape Town and Durban to Fremantle, which altogether took one month, then spent a month ashore in Australia and New Zealand, and then had a month-long voyage home from Auckland to Tahiti, the Panama Canal, Curacao, Trinidad and the Azores. The ship's fare was £890 for two for three months or just under £10 per person per day.

eight

LOUNGING IN THE SUNSHINE: THE AGE OF CRUISING

When, in December 2007, the Duchess of Cornwall, accompanied by the Prince of Wales, named the 90,000-ton, 2,000-berth *Queen Victoria* of Cunard at Southampton, the British-passenger ship business was booming, at its greatest peak in decades. Over 1 million British travellers were taking cruises and many of them on British-owned ships. Cunard, having added the 151,000-ton, 2,600-passenger *Queen Mary 2*, subsequently commissioned the 92,000-ton *Queen Elizabeth* in 2010. Meanwhile, a sister company to Cunard (since both are owned by Miami-based Carnival Corporation), P&O was almost bigger than ever with eleven large cruise ships. In 2010, they were operating the *Arcadia*, *Artemis*, *Aurora*, *Oceana*, *Oriana* and, largest of all, the 116,000-ton, 3,500-bed sisters *Ventura* and *Azura*. In addition, P&O's Australian cruise arm sailed four liners, the *Pacific Dawn*, *Pacific Jewel*, *Pacific Pearl* and *Pacific Sun*.

By the 1960s, cruising on British liners was still rather select, almost special. The pinnacle of cruising for British passengers on a British ship was to sail aboard the *Andes* of the Royal Mail Lines. As Cunard's *Caronia* catered to American travellers, the *Andes* was likened to being a large yacht; she was said to be impeccable. Ron Peach served as a steward aboard her when she ran mostly two- to three-week-long cruises from Southampton. 'She was like a grand, floating country club,' he recalled:

Everything on board was done with great precision, almost according to a gold-trimmed script. Passengers, many of them titled, came year after year, usually requesting the same suite or cabin, the same table in the restaurant and even the same cabin steward and dining room waiter. The *Andes* had an enormous sense of familiarity about her. We catered to about 500 mostly well-heeled passengers with more than 300 select crew and staff to look after them.

Very popular but mass-market cruising in the 1960s was offered by the *Reina Del Mar*, which was operated by Union-Castle Line, and the likes of the *Southern Cross* and *Northern Star* of Shaw Savill.

Some earlier cruise ships were not especially successful, however, and were troubled and received bad press, often for a variety of reasons. 'Shaw Savill's *Northern Star* was absolutely trouble-prone,' according to Tony Ralph:

By the early '70s, when she was cruising fulltime, her mechanical problems seemed to increase. It seemed that no cruise itinerary was ever complete, almost customarily skipping two out of 5 ports of call. This did not go over well with the passengers or enhance Shaw Savill's image and selling potential. The *Northern Star* was just about clinging to dear life in the end! Shaw Savill itself was losing money and cutting back. The results showed. On board maintenance declined sharply. There was rust everywhere, dirty windows in the lounges and along the promenades, and an increasingly unhappy attitude amongst the crew. Once a fine company, Shaw Savill had lost focus and consequently lost interest in the passenger ship business. When the *Northern Star* was sold for scrap [to Taiwanese buyers], at the age of only thirteen, in 1975, the Company all but breathed a sigh of relief. There was no hesitation or sentimentality in selling her.

Unique in style, school-ship cruising was also very popular in the 1960s and '70s. Leslie Shaw took his first school-ship cruise in 1972, aboard the *Nevasa*, where the 300 adult passengers were divided quite separately from the 1,100 youngsters. 'On that first trip, with 900 kids aboard, was a seven-day voyage to La Pallice [France], Vigo and Oporto. We liked this rather unique concept in ocean cruising,' he remembered:

There were excellent lecturers on board and you could always ask questions afterward. There were no professional performers, like the magicians and feathery dancers, but instead the officers entertained. There was also lots of quizzes. Most of the adult passengers tended to be getting-on a bit, but were great fun and very interested in travel for travel's sake. One hundred passengers out of the 300 adults would be teachers and another 50 would be connected to schools …

When we were booked again on the *Nevasa* for 1975, she was suddenly sold for scrapping [due to the sudden increases in fuel oil costs] … We were offered by P&O the alternate of a three-week cruise from Southampton to the Caribbean in the *Oriana*. With 1,700 passengers aboard, she was far too big for our liking. Actually, we saw passengers on the boat train returning to London from Southampton that we hadn't seen on board the ship itself. We returned to school ship cruising, in the *Uganda*, and remained faithful to her until she was requisitioned for service in the Falklands War in 1982. She was our favourite ship and the friendliest.

Then P&O's new flagship, the 69,100grt *Oriana* is seen being floated out from the building shed at the Meyer Werft yard in Papenburg, Germany. This view dates from 30 July 1994. *(Meyer Werft)*

The little 3,100grt *St Helena*, a former Canadian coastal passenger-cargo ship, made line voyages to the South Atlantic and South Africa beginning in 1978. *(St Helena Shipping Co.)*

The 24-knot *Oriana* is outbound on the right with the *Canberra* still berthed on the left at the Queen Elizabeth II Terminal at Southampton. *(Ken Vard Collection)*

The *Pacific Princess*, made especially famous by her role in television's *Love Boat* series, is seen berthed at Lisbon. *(Luis Miguel Correia Collection)*

The 17,500grt *Cunard Princess* berthed at Cozumel with the cruise ship *Vera Cruz I* on the left. *(Cunard)*

The innovative 44,500grt *Royal Princess* is seen during a Scandinavian summer cruise while berthed at Copenhagen. The date is June 1990. *(Ove Neilsen Collection)*

New era: the largest Atlantic liner of all time, the 151,000grt *Queen Mary 2*, is stylishly depicted in this maiden voyage poster. *(Cunard)*

A former troopship, British India Line's 1937-built *Dunera* ran educational cruises during the 1960s. *(Richard Faber Collection)*

Two royal ladies: the *Queen Mary 2* on the left and the *Queen Elizabeth 2* on the right in the first meeting of the two famed liners. The photograph is at New York and dated 25 April 2004. *(Charles Cotton Collection)*

The *Queen Mary 2* is the glorious successor to Cunard's illustrious, transatlantic Queens. *(Author's Collection)*